Words
to Live By

Selected and Interpreted by
Ninety-six Eminent Men and Women
Edited by

William Nichols

REVISED AND ENLARGED EDITION

1949

SIMON AND SCHUSTER

PUBLISHED BY SIMON AND SCHUSTER, INC.

ROCKEFELLER CENTER, 1230 SIXTH AVENUE

NEW YORK 20, N. Y.

SECOND EDITION

SECOND PRINTING

ACKNOWLEDGMENTS

Permission has been granted to reprint the following material:

From *The Summing Up,* copyright 1938, by W. Somerset Maugham; by permission of Doubleday & Company, Inc.

Lines from the poem *Primer Lesson* from *Slabs of the Sunburnt West* by Carl Sandburg, copyright 1922, Harcourt, Brace and Company, Inc.

From *The Bond Between Us* by Frederic M. Loomis; by permission of the author and *The Reader's Digest.* Copyright for *The Bond Between Us* by Frederic M. Loomis was issued to Alfred Knopf, Inc., May, 1942, and transferred by them to the author on August 23, 1946.

Lines from *Poems* by Stephen Spender, copyright 1934, Random House, Inc.

From *TVA—Democracy on the March,* copyright 1944, by David E. Lilienthal; by permission of Harper & Brothers.

From *Peace of Mind,* copyright 1946, by Joshua Loth Liebman; by permission of Simon & Schuster, Inc.

From *The Seven Storey Mountain* by Thomas Merton, copyright 1948, Harcourt, Brace and Company, Inc.

From Secretary Marshall's Alumni Day Address at Princeton University, February 22, 1947.

MANUFACTURED IN THE UNITED STATES OF AMERICA

AMERICAN BOOK—STRATFORD PRESS, INC., NEW YORK

To My Wife

Who taught me that philosophy is not just
a text-book word, but the path to intensified love, intensified living and intensified
common sense.

Contents

Contents

Contents

ix

Contents

Introduction

HOW THIS BOOK CAME TO BE WRITTEN

THIS BOOK IS the flowering of an idea which began as an experiment, and then turned into rare adventure.

It started this way: Some time ago, I was reading a wise, good, quiet book by David Grayson called *Under My Elm,* in which this gentle philosopher told stories about rural life in his New England village with his country neighbors. It was a strangely restful book to read, especially in that year, 1945, when everybody was talking tensely about the "end of our era" and the "doom of our civilization."

One chapter appealed to me especially. In it, Grayson described an old farmer-neighbor who was a kind of walking anthology. Whenever he ran across some bit of verse or prose he liked, this rural collector preserved it, slipped the words inside his hatband, to be tacked up later on his granary wall or the partitions of his horse barn.

"I thought afterward," Grayson wrote, "as I tramped up the town road, how most of us have collections of sayings we live by. . . . I believe it would be difficult to find an adult human being who hasn't a saying or two, or more, that he is saving because it expresses something vital."

That chance paragraph from David Grayson's Amherst study set me to planning a fascinating voyage of discovery, not into barns and granaries, but into the minds and hearts of many people during a period when our world was seemingly plunged in doubt, pessimism and fear.

The quest was to be an editorial venture, for I believed that words which had caught the imagination of one man or woman should be shared with others in the pages of *This Week* Magazine, where nine million families of men and women could make them part of their lives.

The first step was to select a list of people who, through their achievements, were what the world regards as successful. Then, to each of them went a letter which read like this: "These are times when millions of Americans are deeply disturbed and many of them are unhappy. We are surrounded by all the comforts of a machine age, and yet we have somehow lost our sense of the meaning and purpose and beauty of life. Possibly you have faced the same problem. Perhaps you have found some words to live by, and treasured them because they say something which you regard as vital."

The appeal touched a rich source of inspiration. For several years, each issue of *This Week* has opened with "words" which came in in response to my letters, and which then flowed out to bring hope and comfort to others.

At first, each selection, and the comment which accompanied it, seemed to be only a "random" thought—pleasant enough, often inspiring, but with no general significance. But as the weeks went by, and the contributions kept coming in, I suddenly realized that here, in the truest sense, was philosophy in the making. One by one, the people of our time were bringing in to me the wisdom gleaned from their own experience in living. Placed all together these fragments suddenly fell into a thrilling pattern, a rich mosaic—a way of life for our time.

Here, to start with, is one group of men and women, speaking about the things which affect Man in relation to Himself—his happiness, success, fulfillment.

Here is another group speaking of Man and his Society— all the things which go to make up a free and decent way of life.

And here is a group who speak of the most important subject of all—Man and his relation to God.

Man and Himself. Man and Society. Man and God. These are the three elements of living. In this book, a group of men and women talk about them in terms of their own experience, their own wisdom achieved through trial and error. A professional philosopher, no doubt, could find many flaws and lapses in the sections which follow. Yet I present them without apology. On these pages you will meet people who reveal, in their words to live by, what they are feeling and thinking and believing in this atomic age. With them I hope you will recapture, as I have done, a sense of courage and of enduring confidence in the future which lies beyond the uneasy clouds of our time.

WILLIAM NICHOLS

PART ONE

Man
and
Himself

Enjoying
Life

On Morals by Donald Culross Peattie
On Ups and Downs by Willy Pogany
On Good Companions by Charles Hanson Towne
On Laughter by Gelett Burgess
On Having Fun by Frederic Loomis
On Thinking by Helen Keller
Be Happy by Lloyd Morris

On Morals

BY

DONALD CULROSS PEATTIE

AUTHOR AND NATURALIST

"If your morals make you dreary, depend upon it they are wrong."
—ROBERT LOUIS STEVENSON

I HAVE LONG been delighted by this warning from the gallant prophet of the lively creed which declares that to be happy, if you possibly can, is a first duty to others. How the world has suffered from the dreary moralists, those gloomy souls who want to make other people good, rather than happy! They have darkened the lives of children with threats of hell-fire, hanged the witches at Salem, and persecuted thousands. Today, they counsel paralyzing doubt in a world that desperately needs strength of heart.

Stevenson's words do not mean that if your life is dull you must abandon moral standards and seek happiness in

5

self-indulgence. But they do remind us that true goodness is a joyful thing. Men of true morality proclaim courage and gladness, and rouse in us the rapture of living. St. Francis of Assisi, Mozart, Audubon, Don Marquis—there springs to mind a motley company of fellows who knew how to minister to the world, and yet call up from it a laugh and a light heart.

The wind running through the grass, the thrush in the treetops, and children tumbling in senseless mirth stir in us a bright faith in life. It is heresy to turn from them with a frown. Dreary moralizing is poison in a cup of holy water. To live that way is to live by fear, not love. It is to think less of heaven than of hell. Indeed, I believe it is the cardinal irreverence.

On Ups and Downs

BY

WILLY POGANY

ARTIST AND ILLUSTRATOR

"Bear shame and glory with an equal peace and an ever tranquil heart."

—BHAGAVAD-GITA

THESE WORDS FROM the Sacred Book of the Hindus always had a special appeal for me, as I happen to be of a temperamental and impulsive nature. To accept success or disappointment with serene detachment is the stoic philosophy that I have tried to live by: to remain calm in times of great adversity, and to keep a level head if some good fortune came my way. However, there are two exceptions that have existed down through the ages: as I soon found out, all philosophy is useless against love or toothache—and one's life is so full of such.

On Good Companions

BY

CHARLES HANSON TOWNE

POET, AUTHOR, EDITOR AND ACTOR

"So long as we love, we serve; so long as we are loved by others, I should say that we are almost indispensable; and no man is useless while he has a friend."
—ROBERT LOUIS STEVENSON

THE ABOVE WORDS emphasize the greatest things man has in life—love and friendship. They have long been an inspiration to me on cloudy days of spiritual depression. It is good to be reminded of the fact that we are needed by our fellows; that we are more than brothers to the ox; that we are truly of some importance, however small, in a struggling world. It is something to live for others instead of only for ourselves. Indeed, we do not really live unless we have friends surrounding us like a firm wall against the winds of the world.

On Laughter

BY

GELETT BURGESS

HUMORIST AND AUTHOR OF
"THE PURPLE COW"

*"Laffing iz the sensation ov pheeling good all over,
and showing it principally in one spot."*
—JOSH BILLINGS

THE OLD PROFESSOR I went to hear, that night
in Paris, began his talk by commanding: "Laugh! Everybody in the audience laugh! Laugh out loud. That's it. Now
louder! Louder!" One after another began to laugh, and
soon the whole place was convulsed with uproarious laughter.

I hadn't felt much like laughing when I went in. Some
people can laugh at their own troubles, but when one you
love is suffering and you can do nothing to help, it's hard to
show mirth. I had almost forgotten how to smile. But I

9

laughed with the rest—I couldn't help it—and I went away feeling definitely happier.

Next day I saw in a magazine the picture of a sweepstakes winner. She was laughing all over. I pinned her to my wall and every time I looked at her I smiled. Every time, I felt better.

Then I began to cut out every laughing picture I could find, in newspapers, magazines, advertisements. I finally filled a book with them. Not mere photographic smiles or smirks, though. You need genuine, ha-ha-ha laughter to stimulate merriment.

I showed my scrapbook to a nurse. She roared. In the hospital she gave it to a patient, and at sight of those laughing faces, he smiled for the first time in months. From bed to bed the book was passed, and in one ward after another the doctors testified that this laugh cure almost always produced a marked improvement. I made other scrapbooks; I sent them to discouraged or ailing friends, always with the same happy result.

Laughter is a real medicine. It has optimistic vitamins in it. It revives like oxygen. It restores failing morale. I have proved for myself the "cleansing power of laughter."

On Having Fun

BY

FREDERIC LOOMIS

DOCTOR-TURNED-AUTHOR

"Enjoy yourself. It is later than you think."
—CHINESE PROVERB

I HAVE TOLD many times the story of a certain letter which I received years ago, because the impression it made on me was very deep; and I have never told it, on ships in distant seas or by quiet firesides nearer home, without a reflective, thoughtful response from those around me. The letter:

Peking, China

Dear Doctor:

Please don't be too surprised in getting a letter from me. I am signing only my first name. My surname is the same as yours.

You won't even remember me. Two years ago, I was in

your hospital under the care of another doctor. I lost my baby the day it was born.

That same day my doctor came in to see me, and as he left he said, "Oh, by the way, there is a doctor here with the same name as yours who noticed your name on the board, and asked me about you. He said he would like to come in to see you, because you might be a relative. I told him you had lost your baby and I didn't think you would want to see anybody, but it was all right with me."

And then in a little while you came in. You put your hand on my arm and sat down for a moment beside my bed. You didn't say much of anything but your eyes and your voice were kind, and pretty soon I felt better. As you sat there I noticed that you looked tired and that the lines in your face were very deep. I never saw you again but the nurses told me you were in the hospital practically night and day.

This afternoon I was a guest in a beautiful Chinese home here in Peking. The garden was enclosed by a high wall, and on one side, surrounded by twining red and white flowers, was a brass plate about two feet long. I asked someone to translate the characters for me. They said:

Enjoy Yourself
It Is Later Than You Think

I began to think about it for myself. I had not wanted another baby because I was still grieving for the one I lost. But I decided that moment that I should not wait any longer. Perhaps it may be later than I think, too.

And then, because I was thinking of my baby, I thought

of you and the tired lines in your face, and the moment of sympathy you gave me when I so needed it. I don't know how old you are but I am quite sure you are old enough to be my father; and I know that those few minutes you spent with me meant little or nothing to you of course—but they meant a great deal to a woman who was desperately unhappy.

So I am so presumptuous to think that in turn I can do something for you too. Perhaps for you it is later than you think. Please forgive me, but when your work is over, on the day you get my letter, please sit down very quietly, all by yourself, and think about it.

Marguerite

Usually I sleep very well when I am not disturbed by the telephone, but that night I woke a dozen times seeing the brass plate in the Chinese wall. I called myself a silly old fool for being disturbed by a letter from a woman I couldn't even remember, and dismissed the thing from my mind; and before I knew it I found myself saying again to myself: "Well, maybe it is later than you think; why don't you do something about it?"

I went to my office next morning and told them I was going away for three months.

It is a wholesome experience for any man who thinks he is important in his own organization to step out for a few months. The first time I went away on a long trip, some years before this letter came, I felt sure that everything would go to pieces. When I returned I found there were just as many patients as when I left, every one had recovered just as fast or faster, and most of my patients did not even know I had been away. It is humiliating to find how quickly and competently one's place is filled, but it is a very good lesson.

Many years have been added to the average expectation of life but each individual's fate is still a hazard. The most valuable people around us have lived largely for others. This seems the time to remind them that they will have more years, and happier ones, to do good for others if they start right now to do something for themselves; to go places and to do things which they have looked forward to for years; to give those who love them the happiness of seeing them enjoy some of the rewards which they have earned; to replace competition with a bit of contemplation.

On Thinking

BY

HELEN KELLER

DEAF, DUMB AND BLIND
AUTHOR AND LECTURER

"I think, therefore I am."
—DESCARTES

MINE HAS BEEN the limited experience of one who lives in a world without color and without sound. But ever since my student days I have had a joyous certainty that my physical handicaps were not an essential part of my being, since they were not in any way a part of my mind. This faith was confirmed when I came to Descartes' maxim, "I think, therefore I am."

Those five emphatic words waked something in me that has never slept since. I knew then that my mind could be a positive instrument of happiness, bridging over the dark, silent void with concepts of a vibrant, light-flooded happiness. I learned that it is possible for us to create light and sound and order within us, no matter what calamity may befall us in the outer world.

Be Happy!

BY

LLOYD MORRIS

AUTHOR OF

"POSTSCRIPT TO YESTERDAY"

"The days that make us happy make us wise."
—JOHN MASEFIELD

WHEN I FIRST read this line by England's Poet Laureate, it startled me. What did Masefield mean? Without thinking about it much, I had always assumed that the opposite was true. But his sober assurance was arresting. I could not forget it.

Finally, I seemed to grasp his meaning and realized that here was a profound observation. The wisdom that happiness makes possible lies in clear perception, not fogged by anxiety nor dimmed by despair and boredom, and without the blind spots caused by fear.

Active happiness—not mere satisfaction or contentment

—often comes suddenly, like an April shower or the un-folding of a bud. Then you discover what kind of wisdom has accompanied it. The grass is greener, bird songs are sweeter. The shortcomings of your friends are more un-derstandable and more forgivable. Happiness is like a pair of eyeglasses correcting your spiritual vision.

Nor are the insights of happiness limited to what is near around you. Unhappy, with your thoughts turned in upon your emotional woes, your vision is cut short as though by a wall. Happy, the wall crumbles.

The long vista is there for the seeing. The ground at your feet, the world about you—people, thoughts, emo-tions, pressures—are now fitted into the larger scene. Everything assumes a fairer proportion. And here is the beginning of wisdom.

The Road

to

Success

Setting Your Goal

BY

HENRY SEIDEL CANBY

AUTHOR, CRITIC AND AN EDITOR OF
"THE SATURDAY REVIEW OF LITERATURE"

"Our life is frittered away by detail. . . . The nation is ruined . . . by want of calculation and a worthy aim. . . . It lives too fast."

—THOREAU

MILLIONS OF AMERICAN women fritter away their lives by a thousand details of which nine hundred get them nowhere—certainly not toward happiness. And so do their husbands. They live fast, but neither hard nor deep. They live too fast because they don't know where they are going, and so have to hurry to get there. They can't simplify their lives because they have never simplified their thinking. These millions have never stopped long enough to calculate what is an aim worth having. They don't really know what they want.

Henry Thoreau, our greatest natural philosopher, had his own solution to the problem. He wanted to write a book, and so for two years he lived a hermit-like life in the woods, cultivating beans and corn to keep up his rations. He succeeded in escaping from the fritter and the fluster of living in Concord village while he thought out his book and wrote it; then he came home. In short, he found out his worthwhile aim, and then got rid of the particular kinds of detail that frittered away his time and energy.

This doesn't necessarily mean that we must all follow Thoreau's exact example—above all, that is no solution for anyone who hates beans and gardening. But nearly everyone can apply his general principle. We live in the midst of details that keep us running round in circles and never getting anywhere but tired, or that bring on nervous breakdowns and coronary thrombosis. The answer is not to take to the woods, but to find out what we really want to do and then cut out the details that fritter away what is most valuable in life. *Live deep instead of fast.* I think this is what Thoreau meant.

Starting Out

BY

WILLIAM SAROYAN

AUTHOR AND PLAYWRIGHT

"It is not impossible to walk on water."
—GARABED SAROYAN

THESE WORDS WERE said to me about twenty-five years ago by my great-uncle Garabed Saroyan when he came into my bed-living-and-work room in a house in Fresno, California, where I had recently installed a typewriter.

I was almost thirteen at the time and he was an old man. I thought he was as old as any man could be, although he was probably well under sixty.

He said, "My boy, what is that contraption?"

I said, "It is a typewriter, sir."

"What is it for?" he said.

"It is for clear writing," I said, and handed him an example of typewriter-print on paper.

"What is this writing on the paper?"

"Philosophical sayings."

"By which philosopher?" my great-uncle Garabed said.

"By myself," I said.

He sat on the bed, lighted a cigarette, then studied the sheet of paper and his great-nephew.

When he got up to go he said, "Proceed, for it is not impossible to walk on water."

Even though he had said very little, there was no mistaking what he meant. Coming from him, a man famous for his fierce wit, this was approval, recognition and encouragement to keep on trying, and I felt much obliged to him.

Keeping Going

BY

CORNELIA OTIS SKINNER

ACTRESS-MONOLOGIST AND CO-AUTHOR OF
"OUR HEARTS WERE YOUNG AND GAY"

"This day we sailed on. Course WSW."
—CHRISTOPHER COLUMBUS

THIS WAS THE entry which, day after day, Columbus put down in the private log of his first voyage across the uncharted North Atlantic. He must have written it in a spirit alternating between blind hope and quiet despair.

Conditions were about as adverse as possible. Storms had damaged the little caravel; the *Pinta* had lost her rudder; the crews of all three vessels were threatening mutiny; and probably Columbus' own confidence in what seemed an insane enterprise was wavering. But he had set his course in the direction which his own intuition and logical intelligence led him to believe was the right one, and with dogged courage he kept on going.

25

The words are not especially comforting ones, but these are days when the world is less in need of supine comfort than of high gallantry and faith in an inner integrity. During times of distress, doubt and weariness, people may well be inspirited by the words of the great navigator, "This day we sailed on."

Mileposts

BY

DALE CARNEGIE

AUTHOR OF "HOW TO
STOP WORRYING AND START LIVING"

"Anyone can carry his burden, however hard, until nightfall. Anyone can do his work, however hard, for one day."
—ROBERT LOUIS STEVENSON

ONE OF THE most appalling comments on our present way of life is that half of all our hospital beds are occupied by patients with nervous and mental troubles. And a principal cause is that too many people allow themselves to collapse under the crushing burdens of accumulated yesterdays and fearful tomorrows.

Here is the problem: You and I are standing in this split second at the meeting place of two eternities—the vast past that has endured forever and the future that is plunging on to the last syllable of recorded time. We can't possibly live in either of these eternities, but we often try to do so; and, in the process, we wreck both our bodies and our minds.

The answer, as Stevenson says, is to live for today. Of course, it may be that part of today's work calls for reviewing the past, or planning for tomorrow. But there's no excuse for doing so with panic or regret. Instead we should get the facts and push on from there.

Today is the only time we can possibly live. Let's not turn it into a physical and mental hell by aimless worry about the future. Let's also stop fretting over the blunders we made yesterday.

Remember how a walking trip always seems shorter if we concentrate, not on the total distance to our destination, but just the distance to the next milepost. In the same way, we should concentrate on living within today. Then better tomorrows will inevitably follow.

Setbacks

BY

FERENC MOLNAR

NOTED HUNGARIAN PLAYWRIGHT

"Work is the best narcotic!"
—MAURICE MOLNAR

EXACTLY FIFTY YEARS ago my father gave me
the words I have lived by ever since. He was a physician.
I had just started to study law at the Budapest University.
I failed one examination. I thought I could not survive the
shame so I sought escape in the consolation of failure's
closest friend, alcohol, always at hand: apricot brandy to
be exact.

My father called on me unexpectedly. Like a good doctor he discovered both the trouble and the bottle, in a second. I confessed why I had to escape reality.

The dear old man then and there improvised a prescrip-
tion. He explained to me that there can be no real escape
in alcohol or sleeping pills—or in any drug. For any sorrow

29

there is only one medicine, better and more reliable than all the drugs in the world: work!

How right my father was! Getting used to work might be hard. Sooner or later you succeed. It has, of course, the quality of all the narcotics. It becomes habit-forming. And once the habit is formed, sooner or later, it becomes impossible to break one's self of it. I have never been able to break myself of the habit for fifty years.

Faith

BY

ROBERT HILLYER

POET AND TEACHER

"If the Sun and Moon should doubt,
They'd immediately go out."
—WILLIAM BLAKE

AS A POET, I have often wished I could have written these lines. As a teacher, I have often called them to my aid for the encouragement of someone who could not get started on a project. Faith in oneself is an important part of all other faiths. The lack of it can paralyze a life.

Of course it is natural to have nervous moments. Everyone who has spoken in public is acquainted with the panic that seizes one just before the occasion, and we are told that the best actors are those who are most nervous just before the curtain goes up. There is always the fear that lines will be forgotten, that something will go wrong, and yet the play goes on, usually without a hitch.

The same preliminary lack of confidence attends every accomplishment known to man, the launching of a military campaign, the composition of a poem, the salesman's first trip, the bride's cookery. But if we all succumbed to such misgivings, nothing would ever be done.

Self-doubt is caused by the fact that every human activity involves some other person whose praise or blame seems unduly important. We set a goal of perfection before ourselves and groaningly conclude that it cannot be achieved.

But perfectionism is a dangerous state of mind in an imperfect world. The best way is to forget doubts and set about the task in hand. While the battle is being fought or the cake is baking in the oven, leave the outcome to the future where it belongs. If you are doing your best, you will not have time to worry about failure.

Anvil Moments

BY
JAN STRUTHER
AUTHOR OF "MRS. MINIVER"

"When you are an anvil, hold you still;
When you are a hammer, strike your fill."
—JOHN FLORIO

THIS COUPLET, WRITTEN in 1591, expresses
with beautiful economy a deep truth: that in order to live
our lives we need the two balanced but related qualities
of humility and resolution; of patience in suffering and
strength in action. We are both object and subject, both the
slave of fate and its master.

There are some situations in which we are unable to take
action. Losses, bereavements, disappointments, disease—
these may strike at any hour with terrible force. All we can
do is to brace ourselves against the shock. Those are our anvil moments.

But there are other situations in which we have the power to act: and that is when we need all our firmness and singleness of purpose. We must strike quickly, strike hard, and above all strike in the right place.

With these two qualities—patience and strength—we can endure all things, and achieve many.

Enemies

BY

HODDING CARTER

MISSISSIPPI EDITOR
PULITZER PRIZE WINNER

*"Just as tall trees are known by their shadows, so are
good men known by their enemies."*
—OLD CHINESE PROVERB

MOST OF US spend overmuch of our time seeking to
be popular with everyone and fretting because we've heard
that so-and-so doesn't like us. Too often we measure our
standing in our communities by the number of backslaps,
the frequency of party invitations and the relayed reports
of what Bill or Joe or Mary say about us. We are so busy
trying to make friends that we don't take time to make the
right kind of enemies.

Yet one of the saintliest men I ever knew, a lawyer in
a small Southern city, was hated by some of his fellow
citizens with a hate surpassing Cain's for Abel. I know he

took strength from their ill regard; and he once said that he became concerned only when he could not identify the reasons his enemies had for disliking him.

The reasons were almost always evident: a tainted official, seeking to ridicule him for his insistence upon decency in public office. A standpatter, uneasy because of his forthright support of equal rights for racial and religious minorities. A rigid fanatic, aroused because of his gentler and deeper interpretation of moral laws. A suspicious realist, unable to understand a grown man's love of beauty. A careful financier (at eight per cent), decrying his impetuous generosity and disregard for business orthodoxy.

All his life he was libeled, but the attacks left him untouched and undisturbed, and in the long run caused him to be held in honor, respect and affection.

Of course, no one enjoys—or should enjoy—unpopularity as such. But neither should we be afraid of making enemies.

Tall trees must cast long shadows, and the man for whom everyone has a passing good word is but a fraction of a man and empty of purpose.

Face and Fortune

BY

FRANCES PARKINSON KEYES

AUTHOR OF "CAME A CAVALIER"
AND "DINNER AT ANTOINE'S"

"To thine own self be true."
—SHAKESPEARE

THERE IS a story about a proposed appointment in Lincoln's cabinet that I have always liked very much. One of his advisers urgently recommended a candidate and Lincoln declined to follow the suggestion. So he was asked to give his reasons.

"I don't like the man's face," Lincoln explained briefly.

"But the poor man is not responsible for his face," his advocate insisted.

"Every man over forty is responsible for his face," Lincoln replied, and turned to the discussion of other matters.

Recently, at the instigation of my publisher, I had some photographs taken. It was a long time, he reminded me, since I had supplied him with a new one; I could not go on using the same pose indefinitely. I do not enjoy the process of being photographed, and when I saw the results of this latest ordeal, I enjoyed these still less. I compared the new photograph with one that had been taken twenty-five years ago, and my feminine vanity suffered an acute pang at the thought of being presented to the public as I am today. My first instinct was to have the prints "touched up," though I have never "touched up" my own face or my own hair because I have always maintained that women who did this deceived no one except themselves. As I thoughtfully considered the photographs, I knew that a still more important principle was involved.

A quarter century of living should put a great deal into a woman's face besides a few wrinkles and some unwelcome folds around the chin. In that length of time she has become intimately acquainted with pain and pleasure, joy and sorrow, life and death. She has struggled and survived, failed and succeeded. She has lost and regained faith. And, as a result, she should be wiser, gentler, more patient and more tolerant than she was when she was young. Her sense of humor should have mellowed, her outlook should have widened, her sympathies should have deepened. And all this should show. If she tries to erase the imprint of age, she runs the risk of destroying, at the same time, the imprint of experience and character.

I know I am more experienced than I was a quarter century ago and I hope I have more character. I released the pictures as they were.

Praise

BY

PETER B. KYNE

NOVELIST, CREATOR OF THE
"CAPPY RICKS" STORIES

If you think that praise is due him,
Now's the time to slip it to him,
For he cannot read his tombstone
when he's dead.
—BERTON BRALEY

IT MUST HAVE been 35 years ago that a young poet friend of mine sold these lines to a newspaper syndicate. Since then he has become a well-known writer. When my own work began to appear in print, those lines came to mind, for many kind, thoughtful readers wrote to tell me that my work had given them pleasure. One such letter from an unknown reader was prefaced by this old New England saying: "Just praise is a debt and should be paid."

Because my old friend and a total stranger gave me a

modicum of their idealism, I have, during the years since, felt many a thrill of vicarious pleasure by making it a point, when somebody has done work I admire, to write and tell him so. I have been richly rewarded for this simple courtesy in the knowledge that I have given these people a cheer they knew they had earned but never expected to receive! And the reward does not stop there. Often, the practice has resulted in treasured friendships.

And as one grows old, and the old friends take off for The Upper Road, the necessity for securing replacements becomes very apparent. As the shadows lengthen, one re-appraises his assets of love and friendship and finds them priceless.

Arrival

BY

MAURICE MAETERLINCK

PLAYWRIGHT, AUTHOR OF
"THE BLUEBIRD"

"The road is always better than the inn."
—CERVANTES

THESE WORDS BY the great Spanish writer, Cervantes, mean a way of living. In my younger days I often aimed too hard to reach some goal, finish some job. "When this is done," I'd say, "I shall find satisfaction and reward."

But later I came to realize that each achievement, like each inn, is only a point along the road. The real goodness of living comes with the journey itself, with the striving and desire to keep moving. Now I find that I can look back on my eighty-four years with pleasure and, what is even more important to me, that I can still look to the future with hope and desire. I have learned to take each inn along the way with a traveler's stride—not as a stopping point, but a starting point for some new and better endeavor.

Some

Virtues

On Patience

BY

WALTER B. PITKIN

TEACHER, AUTHOR OF
"LIFE BEGINS AT FORTY"

"The most useful virtue is patience."
—JOHN DEWEY

IN THIS ATOMIC age, at the gray dawn of One World, patience is more useful than ever before. It is the supreme modern virtue. Those who practice it succeed and grow happy. Those who flout it come to early grief.

Life grows more and more complex. We have to deal with more and more people and things in planning affairs. But that's an added reason why we should learn to relax and take time out for quiet thinking. This is a high-speed age, with many choices; but the faster we move, the surer it is that haste makes waste.

So master patience more thoroughly than ever before.

On Patience

Teach the young to be patient. Then we shall have around us fewer failures and fewer frustrated souls who have overlooked the best, in their haste to win some quick and trifling pleasure.

On Imagination

BY

SIR HAROLD SPENCER JONES

BRITAIN'S ASTRONOMER ROYAL

"To see a world in a grain of sand,
And heaven in a wild flower,
Hold infinity in the palm of your hand,
And eternity in an hour."
—WILLIAM BLAKE

THESE WORDS, WRITTEN by a poet who was also an artist and a mystic, have always attracted me, because they describe more vividly than any others I know the power of imagination.

The astronomer, surveying the vast depths of space, probing into the distant past to study the evolutions of worlds, and looking forward into the remote future, needs this power, of course. But to it we all owe much that makes life worth living; for all music, art, poetry and drama that are truly great are inspired by imagination working through experience.

Imagination is inherent in our nature: that is why children live in a world of make-believe. But it is a penalty of our modern civilization that routine, example and precept, by which our lives are so much ordered, tend to warp the free play of the imagination. We need to recapture the power of imagination; we shall then find that life can be full of wonder, mystery, beauty and joy.

On Courage

BY

J. EDGAR HOOVER

DIRECTOR OF THE F.B.I.

*"He that loses wealth loses much:
But he that loses courage loses all."*
—CERVANTES

CERVANTES' WORDS AFFIRM that courage is a priceless ingredient of character. The will to do, the tenacity to overcome all obstacles and finish the course, the strength to cling to inexorable ideals, are rooted in courage. It is the outward manifestation of our spiritual development.

I have never seen a courageous criminal. True, some exhibit bravado behind a gun or in the protection of overwhelming numbers, but that is not real courage. I am speaking of the kind which is vital to the preservation and perpetuation of a free nation: the mental and moral courage which drives us to seek truth. It is the kind which enables us to stand by our convictions, to uphold right for the sake of right. It was this courage which built America. This is the high courage we must develop as pioneers of the Atomic Age. In Cervantes' words lie both a challenge and a warning.

On Fair Play

BY

JOSEPHUS DANIELS

STATESMAN, AMBASSADOR,
FORMER SECRETARY OF THE NAVY

"Put yourself in his place!"
—CHARLES READE

THESE WORDS, the title of one of Charles Reade's novels, have remained in my memory for more than half a century. The story tells of an English village at a time when workers believed that the introduction of labor-saving machines meant taking bread out of the mouths of their wives and children. Living in this community was Dr. Amboyne. He was a wise physician who tended alike to mill owner and mill worker, to the mind as well as to the body. And whenever he found one man denouncing another, he always asked the same question: "What would you do if you were in his place?"

Dr. Amboyne's example has influenced me from youth to age. I have tried—with many lapses—to follow it in all association with my fellows. "Put Yourself in His Place," as practiced by the doctor, is, in effect, to live the Golden Rule. It seems to me, as one who has lived a long time, that it was never more needed than now.

On Humor

BY

LIN YUTANG

CHINESE PHILOSOPHER, AUTHOR OF
"THE IMPORTANCE OF LIVING"

"The great man is he who does not lose his child's heart."

—MENCIUS (372–289 B.C.)

MODERN MAN TAKES life far too seriously, and because he is too serious his world is full of troubles. The importance of humor should never be forgotten. For sense of humor changes the quality and character of our entire cultural life.

It seems to me that the worst thing about dictators is their lack of humor. Dictators always look so solemn or pompous or angry. Presidents of democracies smile and the people like it. They know how to relax and laugh at a good joke. But the dictator gets so puffed up with his own importance that he loses all sense of humor and with it all sense of proportion. That is how we get fanatics. Then the trouble begins.

There is a purifying power in laughter—both for individuals and for nations. If they have a sense of humor, they have the key—to good sense, to simple thinking, to a peaceable temper, and to a cultured outlook on the world.

On Knowledge

BY

STRINGFELLOW BARR

PRESIDENT OF ST. JOHN'S COLLEGE
IN ANNAPOLIS

"All men desire by nature to know."
—ARISTOTLE

THIS SENTENCE WAS true when Aristotle wrote it in Greek, over two thousand years ago. But it is also true today. If we could remember how true it is today in plain English, we would be remembering what America is.

All men desire by nature to know. Aristotle is not hedging, the way we are doing. He means all—men and women, rich and poor, black and white, young and old. Of course he met men who seemed not to want knowledge: everybody meets them. He also met men who seemed not to want food. But if a man stops wanting food, there's something the matter with him physically. If he stops wanting to learn, there's something the matter with him mentally. By nature he has to eat—and he has to learn. If he stops eating, his stomach shrinks, his body gets thin, his face gets pale. If he stops learning, his minds shrinks, his thoughts get thin, his talk gets pale—and boring.

Aristotle's sentence is the charter for every school and college in the land. It is the license for every teacher. He is telling us why we Americans want education to be for everybody. He is telling us why we know in our hearts that grownups need it as much as children do—or more. He is reminding us again that people "just naturally" want to learn. And he knows that people just naturally need to be reminded. For—also by nature, alas!—all men forget the things they most desire.

On Stubbornness

BY

GEORGE JEAN NATHAN

DRAMA CRITIC, EDITOR, AUTHOR OF
"THE THEATRE BOOK OF THE YEAR"

*"You are stubborn and I am going to spank you,
but don't take the spanking too seriously; stubbornness may be one of man's most valuable assets."*
—CHARLES NARÉT-NATHAN

THIS IS THE earliest piece of advice that my father, now
gone these many years, imparted to me. I was about six at
the time and I have no doubt that his reflection on my nature was correct and that he was entirely justified in whaling
the seat off me. Nevertheless, my talent for cussedness has
persisted and even today I sometimes have to scold myself,
though apparently to no avail.

While I appreciate that orneriness is not a trait likely to
win friends or influence people, I wouldn't trade it for a
gold mine. Father was right—a set jawbone is as profitable

to a man in my trade as it is to some other fellow in commerce, prize fighting, matrimony, or any other such hazardous profession.

Stubbornness, true, may be futile, if it proceeds merely from foolish pigheadedness. But it is precious and practical when it is the result of decision filtered through trial and error and when sharp critical analysis gives it body. Then, let them spank you all they wish to, but stick to your guns and you will, God with you, capture the hill.

On Courtesy

BY

FRANK S. HOGAN

DISTRICT ATTORNEY OF NEW YORK COUNTY

*"Hail the small sweet courtesies of life, for smooth
do they make the road of it."*
—LAURENCE STERNE

COURTEOUS TREATMENT IS a recognition by
one person that another person has the same dignity as a
human being. The practice of courtesy develops the habit
of treating others as equals. It is, therefore, more than a
lubricant which prevents irritation between individuals of
different backgrounds. It becomes a solvent of the causes
of friction and, when constantly applied, produces a positive force in the creation of good will.

Is that a little thing? If so, life is full of little things—
full of small pains and petty grievances which little reme-
dies can cure.

It was a little thing which caused the first brothers to quarrel. Abel, you remember, had killed a lamb and brought it as a sacrifice to Jehovah. Cain, in turn, placed some grain on his own altar. The lamb was the more acceptable offering. Cain thought Abel was laughing at him. Abel denied it. Then Cain asked his brother to go away. Abel refused. Whereupon Cain hit Abel. But he hit him too hard, and Abel fell dead.

Fully half of the cases in our criminal courts, where the offense is against the person, originate in little things. Barroom bravado, domestic wrangling, an insulting remark, a disparaging word, a rude action—those are the *little* things that lead to assault and murder.

Very few of us are cruelly and greatly wronged. It is the small blows to our self-esteem, the indignities, the little jolts to our vanity which cause half the heartaches in the world.

If ordinary civility, the courtesy we expect to be shown, were extended to every person with whom we come in contact in our daily lives, would it not be a real contribution to human brotherhood?

On Simplicity

KENNETH ROBERTS

AUTHOR OF "NORTHWEST PASSAGE"
AND "LYDIA BAILEY"

"Beware of all enterprises that require new clothes."

—THOREAU

I WISH THE world, the workers in it, the employers in it, could live by the advice of Thoreau, that social outcast. . . . Here are some other things he said:

"Our life is frittered away by detail. Simplify, simplify!"

"Most of the luxuries, and many of the so-called comforts, of life are not only not indispensable, but positive hindrances to the elevation of mankind."

"If a man does not keep pace with his companions, perhaps it is because he hears a different drummer. Let him step to the music which he hears, however measured or far away."

"If one advances confidently in the direction of his

dreams, and endeavors to live the life which he has imagined, he will meet with a success unexpected in common hours."

How workers in any field of endeavor can accomplish their purposes *without* following Thoreau is beyond my understanding—and I don't believe any of them ever do.

On Enthusiasm

BY

DOUGLAS MACARTHUR

GENERAL OF THE ARMY

GENERAL MAC ARTHUR *chose the following quotation as his Words To Live By, early in the Pacific war. Wherever his headquarters, he placed over his desk three frames—one a portrait of Washington; one a portrait of Lincoln; and between them, the message printed below. It is based on a passage which appeared originally in the book "From the Summit of Years Four Score," by Samuel Ullman of Birmingham, Alabama:*

"Youth is not a time of life; it is a state of mind; it is not a matter of rosy cheeks, red lips and supple knees; it is a matter of the will, a quality of the imagination, a vigor of the emotions; it is the freshness of the deep springs of life.

"Youth means the predominance of courage over timidity, of adventure over the love of ease. This often exists in a man of sixty more than in a boy of twenty. Nobody grows old merely by a number of years. We grow old by deserting our ideals.

"Years may wrinkle the skin, but to give up enthusiasm wrinkles the soul. Worry, doubt, self-distrust, fear and despair—these bow the heart and turn the spirit back to dust.

"Whether sixty or sixteen, there is in every human being's heart the love of wonder, the sweet amazement at the stars and the starlike things, the undaunted challenge of events, the unfailing child-like appetite for what-next, and the joy of the game of living.

"You are as young as your faith, as old as your doubt; as young as your self-confidence, as old as your fear; as young as your hope, as old as your despair."

On Loyalty

BY

HARVEY N. DAVIS

PRESIDENT,
STEVENS INSTITUTE OF TECHNOLOGY

"Unless you can find some sort of loyalty, you cannot find unity and peace in your active living."
—JOSIAH ROYCE

NOWADAYS, when an FBI man asks me about the loyalty of so-and-so, I reply that, as far as I know, he is not, and has never been, and, in my opinion, is not likely to become, either a traitor, a spy, or a Communist of the Russian brand trying to bore from within. That seems to cover the question.

But surely, this adds up to a very narrow definition of the fine old word "loyalty"; and maybe this is a good time for us to re-discover the broader meaning which Professor Royce had in mind, forty years ago, when he wrote the lines quoted above.

On Loyalty

True loyalty, according to Royce's definition, is never a negative thing. It is a positive, wholehearted and outflowing devotion to something beyond your private self, bigger than you are.

In the long run, he believed, no one can be secure or successful or happy if he lives only for himself. We grow only by giving the best of ourselves to something that we believe in heart and soul. This is the essence of loyalty.

In terms of this definition, how loyal are you? Here is a simple way to find out. Below are some things in which nearly everyone believes:

1. Your family
2. The organization for which you work
3. Your community
4. Your church
5. Your country

Now put this list aside. Then take it out again a few days or weeks or months from now. When you do, ask yourself this question: "Since first reading this page, have I so lived that these five things are stronger, better, finer because of me?"

If you can answer a truthful yes, then you will know that you understand the meaning of loyalty—and, along with it, the secret of true happiness.

Some

Vices

On Motes and Beams

BY

W. SOMERSET MAUGHAM

AUTHOR OF "OF HUMAN BONDAGE"

"How seldom we weigh our neighbor in the same balance with ourselves."

—THOMAS À KEMPIS

IT IS CURIOUS that our own offenses should seem so much less heinous than the offenses of others. I suppose the reason is that we know all the circumstances that have occasioned them and so manage to excuse in ourselves what we cannot excuse in others. We turn our attention away from our own defects, and when we are forced by untoward events to consider them, find it easy to condone them. For all I know we are right to do this; they are part of us and we must accept the good and bad in ourselves together.

But when we come to judge others, it is not by ourselves as we really are that we judge them, but by an image that we have formed of ourselves from which we have left out everything that offends our vanity or would discredit us in the eyes of the world. To take a trivial instance: how scornful we are when we catch someone out telling a lie; but who can say that he has never told not one, but a hundred?

There is not much to choose between men. They are all a hotchpotch of greatness and littleness, of virtue and vice, of nobility and baseness. Some have more strength of character, or more opportunity, and so in one direction or another give their instincts freer play, but potentially they are the same. For my part, I do not think I am any better or any worse than most people, but I know that if I set down every action in my life and every thought that has crossed my mind, the world would consider me a monster of depravity. The knowledge that these reveries are common to all men should inspire one with tolerance to oneself as well as to others. It is well also if they enable us to look upon our fellows, even the most eminent and respectable, with humor, and if they lead us to take ourselves not too seriously.

On Pettiness

BY

ANDRÉ MAUROIS

AUTHOR OF "THE ART OF LIVING"

"Life is too short to be little."
—DISRAELI

MY FAVORITE QUOTATION is the sentence above, written by Disraeli. It has helped through many a painful experience.

Often we allow ourselves to be upset by small things we should despise and forget. Perhaps some man we helped has proved ungrateful . . . some woman we believed to be a friend has spoken ill of us . . . some reward we thought we deserved has been denied us. We feel such disappointments so strongly that we can no longer work or sleep. But isn't that absurd?

Here we are on this earth, with only a few more decades to live, and we lose many irreplaceable hours brooding over grievances that, in a year's time, will be forgotten by us and by everybody. No, let us devote our life to worthwhile actions and feelings, to great thoughts, real affections and enduring undertakings. For life is too short to be little.

On Envy

BY

JONATHAN DANIELS

JOURNALIST AND WRITER, AUTHOR OF
"A SOUTHERNER DISCOVERS THE SOUTH"

---

*"Let not him who is houseless pull down the house
of another, but let him work diligently and build
one for himself, thus by example assuring that his
own shall be safe from violence when built."*
—ABRAHAM LINCOLN

IN THESE strife-torn times, men's hopes are often
coupled with their hates. So it is good to remember this
simple philosophy which Lincoln brought from the frontier
to use in a little speech which he made in 1864 to a labor
union.

The words are not often brought forward in our times.
Workers and employers have been too busy seeking the
testimony of their own evident partisans to pause much
over the wholeness of such wisdom for both of them.

Mr. Lincoln was not worried about divisions between workers and employers because he was so honestly simple that he could not see them as separate groups. He had built houses and knew something about the labor involved in the process. He held as worthy of security the things he had helped to make.

Abe Lincoln knew—and maybe he learned it lifting logs —that the laborer is worthy of his hire and that honest hire must include not only bread for today but also hope for tomorrow.

Mr. Lincoln said it very simply: the house and the builder, the bread and the hope, the labor and the security, are not parts in a quarrel but equal elements in the creative enterprise of Americans. And he who does not guard his fellow's security is diligently engaged only in the destruction of his own.

On Vanity

BY

ERIC JOHNSTON

BUSINESS LEADER,
AUTHOR OF "WE'RE ALL IN IT"

"He is truly great that is little in himself and that maketh no account of any height of honors."
—THOMAS À KEMPIS

THE PLAGUE OF the world has ever been the men of vast conceit and vanity—war lords, terrorists, despots and plunderers of the public wealth—who purchased glory for themselves at the price of misery and despair for others.

But lasting good has always been wrought by those who answer to Thomas à Kempis's description, and see themselves infinitely small—as a man feels when he stands alone in darkness, looking up to the starry skies.

It is our failing that we often become confused as to the true meaning of greatness. Too many of the long chapters in history books belong to tyrants and conquerors; too many of the short paragraphs to the healers, the teachers and the servants of truth.

In the long run, the truly great are men of compassion, humility and quiet wisdom. They remember always that they live but a little while, and among men of the same flesh and blood as their own. And this thought must remain with them constantly—regardless of deeds performed, or honors achieved.

On Bluffing

BY

SIDNEY SHALETT

JOURNALIST AND AUTHOR

" . . . They always talk who never think."
—MATTHEW PRIOR

RARE INDEED is the person who never has committed the folly of talking before thinking. As a young reporter, I remember an old editor who used to tell me never to be ashamed to confess ignorance—never to try to cover up lack of knowledge by glib patter.

This wise man used to recall how he had learned the lesson the hard way. Once (as he told it) while crossing the Atlantic, he was approached by a fellow passenger.

"I just wanted to tell you," the man said, and it was obvious he was speaking with considerable emotion, "how deeply I appreciated your message."

Now, the editor could not recall the occasion for any

message; in fact, he could not even place the man who seemed so grateful. But rather than admit he was at a loss, he said rather grandly:

"Oh, that's all right. I was glad of the opportunity to send it."

Naturally, he was puzzled when the other man turned absolutely white and left abruptly without another word.

"On making discreet inquiries," the old editor confessed, "I learned that I knew the man, indeed, and that the message I had been 'so glad to send' him had been one of condolence on the recent death of his wife!"

How many of us have been similarly shamed by stupid errors of the tongue! How many potential friends have we alienated by tactless, hair-trigger references to death, divorce, physical peculiarities or other delicate subjects, spoken without thought in the presence of others to whose backgrounds we were strangers. How easy to avoid all this by thinking first, talking later! After all, even the clam has a better reputation than the magpie.

On Selfishness

BY

JOHN MASON BROWN

CRITIC AND AUTHOR

"This is the true joy in life, the being used for a purpose recognized by yourself as a mighty one; the being thoroughly worn out before you are thrown on the scrap heap; the being a force of Nature instead of a feverish selfish little clod of ailments and grievances complaining that the world will not devote itself to making you happy."
—GEORGE BERNARD SHAW
Preface to *Man and Superman*

WHAT HAPPINESS IS, no person can say for another. But no one, I am convinced, can be happy who lives only for himself. The joy of living comes from immersion in something—more accurately, anything—that we know to be bigger, better, more enduring and worthier than we are. People; ideas; causes; above all continuities—these offer the one possible escape not merely from selfishness but from the hungers of solitude and the sorrows of aimlessness.

No person is as uninteresting as a person without interests. The pitiful people are those who in their living elect to be spectators rather than participants; the tragic ones are those sightseers who turn their backs deliberately on the procession.

Existence is a strange bargain. Life owes us little; we owe it everything. The only true happiness comes from squandering ourselves for a purpose.

On Giving Up

BY

DOROTHY CANFIELD FISHER

AUTHOR AND CRITIC

"Never despair. But if you do, work on in despair."
—EDMUND BURKE

IT WAS OUT of hopeless pain that old Burke sounded that trumpet note. His heart was broken by the death of his adored son; his whole soul darkened by seeing, as he thought, civilization crumbling around him. Many great thinkers have handed down to us some such call to courage. For me, none brings such steadfast help as these words of Edmund Burke. For most of the others picture life as a battle, and cry out to us "Fight on."

But the trouble is that very few can meet life's crises in one short, exalted hour of fighting. Burke knew better. He knew despair as most of us must face it, dragging on through day after dreary day. So he wrote "Work on."

And he was right. With folly and evil triumphant in the

world, we can no more, without shame, fold our hands and sink into despair, than the good soldier on a stricken field can throw his sword away and run for shelter.

Burke was wise, too. For no one of us can possibly know all the forces acting in each human situation. Perhaps in the next town to ours—in the very next house it might be— is someone unknown to us, who is also ready to despair, but who keeps on working. And beyond him, another and yet others—each digging to undermine the foundations of the Dark Tower of wrong. Who knows—perhaps even today, all of us working for what we believe in, have almost undermined those foundations. Perhaps tomorrow the tower will fall.

On Making Mistakes

BY

HELENA KUO

AUTHOR OF "I'VE COME A LONG WAY" AND "GIANTS OF CHINA"

"The sages do not consider that making no mistakes is a blessing. They believe, rather, that the great virtue of man lies in his ability to correct his mistakes and continually to make a new man of himself."

—WANG YANG-MING

THIS SAYING BY a Chinese philosopher and statesman of the fifteenth century has given me hope and cheer in many a personal crisis. Often I suffer agonies of spirit when I realize I have made an enormous and terrible mistake. The whole world seems to be pointing a finger at me and mocking. I can no longer sleep, work or eat. I wish I were dead.

But why should one suffer the tortures of self-fabricated

hell over something that can be corrected? I have erred once, but I shall not do so again. Nothing is gained by wasting time in regretting mistakes. It is much better to employ that time in analyzing and correcting what is wrong.

The greatness of man does not lie in his being faultless. Error is sometimes inevitable. Real virtue lies in recognizing that faults can be set right and in striving to correct them. From the willingness to make such an effort, there must emerge a new and better individual.

On Wishful Thinking

BY

OMAR N. BRADLEY

CHAIRMAN, JOINT CHIEFS OF STAFF

"Make us to choose the harder right instead of the easier wrong, and never to be content with a half truth when the whole can be won."

—COL. C. E. WHEAT

THESE WORDS FROM the West Point Cadet's Prayer contain a warning of two of the worst pitfalls into which men—beset by events—can fall: the loose, wishful thinking that causes some people to hide themselves from the facts; and the willingness to compromise principles for expedient gain.

Wishful thinking is the easy and smoothly paved road to compromise. Knowing that the right road is also the harder one, we have an all-too-human tendency to choose the easier way. And, of course, the justification for our choice becomes a simple task. For we have great powers of rationalization when it comes to proving to ourselves that we have made either a "reasonable" or a "practical" choice.

However, when we choose the easy way out of a difficult decision, we are only running away from reality.

It is a form of daydreaming, and sooner or later we are rudely awakened from the folly of our escape. History has shown time and time again that we have arrived at catastrophe by our failure to respond to events before they have become perilous crises.

If the world is ever to become the peaceful world we want it to be, we must be prepared to live by principles—to pursue those principles completely and without reservation.

We must accept reality and react promptly to all the facts —not only to those we want to hear. And we must fight constantly for the whole truth. For peace can come only from truth, knowledge and honest understanding. Half the truth will produce only half a peace—and half a peace is no longer enough.

On Pride

BY

INGRID BERGMAN

STAGE AND SCREEN STAR

"Look out how you use proud words.
When you let proud words go, it is not easy to call
*   them back.*
They wear long boots, hard boots . . .
Look out how you use proud words."
            —CARL SANDBURG

THERE IS IN these words a primary lesson for individuals and classes and nations alike. All too often, we say the cruel and destructive things—because it is so much easier to be clever than to be kind. But in the long run, proud and angry words are the ones which cause trouble in our homes, our communities and among nations.

Proud words are arrogant, intolerant and savagely ignorant of the great fundamental truths—simplicity, humility and ordinary human decency. They are indeed roughshod, and it is not easy to call them back.

On Prejudice

BY

ELMER DAVIS

NEWS ANALYST,
FORMER DIRECTOR OF THE OWI

"We must take the nations of the world as they are, the human passions and prejudices of peoples as they exist, and find some way to secure . . . a peaceful world."

—GEORGE C. MARSHALL

THIS OBSERVATION, made by our former Secretary of State while he was still a military leader, is something that every American—and every citizen of other self-governing nations, too—must learn to live by if the world is to find peace and stability.

In the late war millions of Americans went abroad, visiting nearly every country in the world. They found that foreigners are different; and in most cases they interpreted that difference to mean that foreigners are inferior—forgetting that the foreigners felt that we were different, and were apt to draw the same conclusion about us.

It would be a far easier world to live in if all nations had the same psychology, the same presuppositions; but they do not—and any intelligent effort to live in a world where no nation can any longer live alone must start from that premise. We can go forward hopefully only if we build on the solid recognition that things are as they are, not as we should like to have them; and if we try to find bases for harmony and cooperation in spite of the differences between nations.

PART TWO

Man
and His
Society

Out of the

Past

Heirlooms and Memories

BY

ROY CHAPMAN ANDREWS

AUTHOR, EXPLORER AND SCIENTIST

*"All true civilization is ninety per cent heirlooms
and memories—an accumulation of small but precious deposits left by the countless generations that
have gone before us. Only very proud or very ignorant people imagine that our muddle-headed present can begin everything all over again every day
—and invent a new alphabet, a new multiplication
table, a new code of laws, and a new religion."*
—REVEREND ROBERT I. GANNON, S. J.
Former President, Fordham University

FATHER GANNON'S WORDS have a meaning
for all of us who want to help make the world a better
place. They remind us that in every field—art, science, in-
dustry or religion—we have a legacy reaching back thousands of centuries—to the man who first drew a picture on
a cave wall; made the first wheel; fashioned the first in-

strument of metal; or raised his eyes in worship to the stars. The progress of civilization has been uneven, but every generation can add something, be it little or much, to this heritage of the past. And today we face the greatest challenge history has ever known. Each one of us is a trustee of the past; we have the task of living up to our heritage—and adding something to it.

Heroes

BY

LOUIS UNTERMEYER

POET, CRITIC, EDITOR OF
'A TREASURY OF GREAT POEMS'

*"I think continually of those who were truly
    great. . . .
The names of those who in their lives fought for
    life,
Who wore at their hearts the fire's center.
Born of the sun they traveled a short while towards
    the sun,
And left the vivid air signed with their honor.*
            —STEPHEN SPENDER

GREATNESS HAS ALWAYS been a mark to aim at.
In these rudderless days, when we are misguided by small
and fumbling minds, it is not only inspiring but impera-
tive to "think continually of those who were truly great."

Soldiers on forgotten fields of battle, scientists in make-
shift laboratories, stubborn idealists fighting to save a lost
cause, teachers who would not be intimidated, tireless doc-

tors, the anonymous army of dreamers and doers—all these by their very living fought for everyone. They sacrificed hours of ease for our casual comforts; they gave up safety for our security. Glorifying the heroic spirit of man, they added to our stature.

Out of the shaken world which surrounds us, Spender reminds us of the unsung champions, the strugglers and pioneers who were inflamed with a burning belief in humanity. It is these fire-bringers, children of light—"born of the sun"—who brought light out of darkness, faith out of confusion, and, leaving "the vivid air signed with their honor," conferred upon us their heritage of hope.

The Real Wisdom

BY

CARL CARMER

FOLK HISTORIAN,
AUTHOR OF "AMERICA SINGS"

"Better a kind fool than a proud wise man."
—English
" 'Mean to' don't pick no cotton." —Negro
"Talk does not cook rice." —Chinese
"A half-truth is a whole lie." —Yiddish
"All are not hunters that blow the horn."—French
"A little too late, much too late." —German
"Giving advice to a fool is like giving medicine to a dead man." —American
"He who knows little, soon repeats it."—Spanish
"The cat is a lion to the mouse." —Albanian
"Who gossips to you will gossip of you."—Turkish

NOT ALL OF man's wisdom has come from the great. The people in the slow passing of the generations have also learned to express truths—truths proved by their own experience. Using their simple vernacular they create sayings that have been sifted and polished by thousands of retellings until they have reached the ultimate in succinct meaning. From the simplicity and brevity of a proverb which has been affirmed by a community-as-a-whole on its journey through time, comes beauty that is not often rivaled by individual literary craftsmen.

The Common Bond
BY
SAMUEL HOPKINS ADAMS
NOVELIST AND BIOGRAPHER

"I am a man; nothing that concerns mankind is alien to me."

—TERENCE

THIS SAYING, for me, is touched with fire. It is as significant today as when its author wrote it in Rome twenty-one centuries ago.

It has a strange origin, that pronouncement of Terence. Born a slave and raised to a class and a nationality whose imperial boast was, "I am a Roman; the world belongs to me," the youthful comedian was the first to affirm the principle of a common kinship. His message came down the ages. Jesus Christ preached it. Milton and Walt Whitman caught and carried on its spirit. Thomas Paine paraphrased it. Pope and Tennyson turned it into living verse. No man ever bettered its utterance.

Never before has the message of solidarity been so

gravely needed. We are living at a time when creeds and ideologies vary and clash. But the gospel of human sympathy is universal and eternal.

Our Good Earth

BY

STUART CHASE

ECONOMIST AND WRITER

"This is our world."
—PAUL B. SEARS

IN THESE FOUR words from a distinguished naturalist are neatly compressed the two great tasks of mankind down the ages. They are also tasks for the individual down the years of his allotted span.

The first is to come to terms with nature.

The second is to come to terms with one's fellows.

The problem was expressed again, though without words, in that stupendous photograph of our earth, taken 100 miles in the air from a V2. Here on that great curve below the mist is our only home. If we abuse it—destroy its soils by erosion, lay waste its cover of forest and grassland, exterminate its wild life, pollute its waters, overturn the balance of nature—our world cannot long protect and support us. Huge fertile areas have already become deserts.

The second task is an even greater challenge. With the bomb now loose, we have learned how to die together, perhaps to the last man. But no Einstein has yet devised a formula to show us how to live together. We had better all turn into Einsteins on this problem—in Washington, in Moscow, at Lake Success, by our own firesides. There isn't much more time.

Ideas

BY

JOHN DEWEY

PHILOSOPHER AND TEACHER

"When men have realized that time has upset many fighting faiths, they may come to believe that the ultimate good is better reached by free trade in ideas."

—OLIVER WENDELL HOLMES

THERE NEVER HAS been a time when it was as important as it is today to take into our heads the spirit that inspires these words. In a time of extreme distress and uncertainty, we reach out blindly for some final and finished truth. Justice Holmes reminds us that truth is a matter of never-ending search. In a time of longing for external authority, he reminds us that the open mind, manifested in free search and free discussion, is the sole method of conducting the search with safety and assurance. In a time when reasonableness and intelligence are undergoing eclipse, he reminds us that fact, discovered by continued inquiry, is in the long run the only ground upon which realization of human desires can be attained.

Action

BY

GEORGE C. MARSHALL

FORMER SECRETARY OF STATE

*"Man is born to act. To act is to affirm the worth
of an end, and to affirm the worth of an end is to
create an ideal."*
—JUSTICE OLIVER WENDELL HOLMES

WHEN IMMEDIATE peril is not plainly visible, there
is a natural tendency to relax and to return to business as
usual, politics as usual, pleasure as usual. People become
indifferent to what I might term the long-time dangers to
their security. The public appears generally in the attitude
of a spectator—interested, yes, but whose serious thinking
is directed to local, immediate matters. Spectators of life are
not those who retain their liberties.

There are many who deplore, but few who are willing to
act—to act directly or to influence political action. Action
depends upon conviction, and conviction in turn depends
upon understanding—a general understanding of the past
history of man on this globe and an understanding that
action is a basic necessity of man's nature.

America's

Promise

The Nature of Democracy by Roger Baldwin
The Promise by Herbert Agar
"Who's Next?" by John R. Tunis
"What Can He Do?" by Samuel Goldwyn
Free Speech by Arthur Garfield Hays
The Common Man by Carl Van Doren
The Uncommon Man by Herbert Hoover
The Danger by Aldous Huxley
The Heritage by Ralph Barton Perry

The Nature of Democracy

ROGER BALDWIN

DIRECTOR OF THE
AMERICAN CIVIL LIBERTIES UNION

---

1. *"Congress shall make no law respecting an establishment of religion, or prohibiting the free exercise thereof; or abridging the freedom of speech or of the press; or the right of the people peaceably to assemble, and to petition the Government for a redress of grievances. . . ."*
2. *"The right of the citizens of the United States to vote shall not be denied or abridged by the United States or by any State on account of race, color, or previous condition of servitude."*
—CONSTITUTION OF THE UNITED STATES

NOT ONLY THE Founding Fathers but the authors of the Four Freedoms and the architects of the United Nations agree in principle that a political democracy lives only by freedom of its citizens to speak, publish, worship and organize without interference. These rights to hear, read, shape public policies and change our government are stated in forthright language in the First Amendment to our Constitution, quoted in the first paragraph above. The second paragraph, from the Fifteenth Amendment, assures the principle of political freedom for all.

These two statements, taken together, are the foundations of our democratic system. They insure control by a majority, with continuing rights of minority opposition. No other political principle has ever been established which so guarantees both stability and orderly change. A world still largely undemocratic has not only the need of these essential guarantees in words, but of the practices they promote. They underlie any concept of an international democracy based on law.

The Promise

BY

HERBERT AGAR

EDITOR, AUTHOR OF
"A TIME FOR GREATNESS"

"After all, there is but one race—humanity."
—GEORGE MOORE

EVERY CIVILIZATION RESTS on a set of promises: moral promises about how to behave toward each
other, physical promises about how to use our economic
system. If the promises are broken too often, the civilization
dies, no matter how rich it may be, or how mechanically
clever. Hope and faith depend on the promises; if hope and
faith go, everything goes.

We Americans have promised each other to treat our
neighbors as equals. The promise rests on our old creed that
every man has in him something of the divine, some spark
of the eternal, which gives him as much right to be taken
seriously as every other man.

This is a noble promise, and from it has come our liberty,

III

and such democracy as we possess; but it must be expressed in terms of action, of something we can all do every day.

Here is something definite which we can all do. We can do it without passing a law, without running for office, without founding a committee. We can do it on our own, without asking anybody's permission.

We can start today by treating each other—rich and poor, Jew and Irishman, Mexican and Chinese, Negro and white —as if we believed in the basic promise which is America.

"Who's Next?"

BY

JOHN R. TUNIS

SPORTSWRITER-TURNED-AUTHOR

THE SHIRT-SLEEVED MAN standing beside the barber chair flipped the apron twice and turned to the three customers sitting by the wall. Again he called out:

"Who's next?"

One of the men put down his paper, rose, took off his coat, hung it on the wall and slipped into the chair. The other two paid no attention. They went on reading.

Just as simple as that. The governor, the bank president, the workman are all equal in the eyes of the law and the barber. Yet this scene that takes place every day in every village, town and city in the United States is the essence of democracy . . . of respect for the rights of other men . . . of co-operation . . . of decency and fair play.

Listen to the two men who are waiting. One is reading the sports pages. After a while he puts the paper down.

"Looks like the Cards will breeze in."

"You mean the Dodgers."

"The Dodgers! You're crazy. The Cards are the team with the pitchers."

"Well, okay. You're entitled to your opinion. This is a free country."

"Who's next?" . . . "This is a free country." . . . You have heard the words a thousand times. So have I. So has every person in this country. Heard them without thinking. Without realizing that this scene and these phrases that we take for granted are part of the deep concepts of a democratic nation. You would never hear them said in lands ruled by totalitarian leaders. There the boss is always right; he can't be questioned. Nor would you hear many other statements we use in our daily life:

"First come, first served."

"He's got his rights."

"May the best man win."

"Give him a break."

"Fair and square."

These expressions are verbal symbols. They mean something to every American. In fact they register to every human being no matter where he lives. They are the everyday Words to Live By of a democracy.

"What Can He Do?"

BY

SAMUEL GOLDWYN

HOLLYWOOD PRODUCER

" . . . America, where people do not inquire of a stranger, 'What is he?' but 'What can he do?' "
—BENJAMIN FRANKLIN

I FIRST CAME upon those words from Franklin's "Information for Those Who Would Remove to America," many years ago in England as a boy of twelve. Relatives of mine had settled in England, but Franklin's comment, which I saw in a reader from which I was studying English, crystallized in me the feeling that the trail of opportunity led farther west—to America.

There has never been a day in my life since then that the eternal truth of that statement has not been borne into me. This is not only "information for those who would remove to America," but deep truth to guide everyone born here as well. For nowhere in the world is the individual the master of his destiny as he is in America.

Here lies opportunity unparalleled in the history of the world, provided that one does not overlook the place where it is to be found—within oneself. True, opportunity exists in the market place all around us, but only if one has or builds within himself the capacity to seek, to find and to develop the possibilities that are waiting, ready to be grasped.

And let no one say that the chances in the future are less than those of the past. For all of its greatness, America has still not attained its maximum development and the years ahead bear greater promise than ever for the young people of the nation.

It is perhaps sentimentality to confess that on my first day in America, I literally kissed the welcoming earth of the land to which I had come. But it is a sentimentality of which I am not ashamed, for as long as I live I shall never cease to give thanks that there exists on the troubled globe one country where freedom and opportunity are denied to no man.

Free Speech

BY
ARTHUR GARFIELD HAYS

DISTINGUISHED LAWYER,
CHAMPION OF CIVIL LIBERTIES

"I disapprove of what you say, but I will defend to the death your right to say it."

—VOLTAIRE

MANY PEOPLE DO not believe in free speech; they believe in "free speech but. . . ." Yet our belief has no meaning unless we are tolerant of utterances we loathe as well as of those we approve.

Is there a line to be drawn anywhere when it comes to expression of opinion? Of course there is, but we must define it carefully. The line should be drawn at the point where words contribute directly to violation of law or to violence. In short, my right to swing my arm ends where the other fellow's nose begins.

Too often, we are inclined to do something to suppress opinions just because we do not like them, whether they be Communist or Fascist doctrine, or anti-Negro, anti-Catholic, anti-Semitic publications and speech. The purpose may be all right, but the philosophy is bad. In order to fulfill an immediate end, we are likely to forget the underlying principle that every human being has an inalienable right to express himself—whether we agree with him or not.

The important point is this: *Free speech works;* it works better in our country than any form of censorship or suppression. We must cherish it carefully. For as long as *everyone* has the right to speak, the truth is bound to emerge. The meaning of our Constitution was never better phrased than in the American colloquialism: "Let 'em talk. This is a free country, isn't it?" It takes faith in this principle to be a good American.

The Common Man

BY

CARL VAN DOREN

HISTORIAN AND BIOGRAPHER

"I know no safe depositary of the ultimate powers of society but the people themselves; and if we think them not enlightened enough to exercise their control with a wholesome discretion, the remedy is not to take it from them, but to inform their discretion by education."

—THOMAS JEFFERSON

THE AGE of Dictators through which we have recently passed confirms again this first principle of Jefferson: the principle that in the long run the people can be trusted to know and find what government is best for them. I know many persons who believe that any such confidence in the people is a mere mystical faith, without support in reality. But the longer I study the behavior of men, past and present, the more I am convinced that government moves in the direction of self-government much as water seeks its own level.

Despots and dictators may for a time constrict the will of the people, as engineers may dam up water. The will of the people may, by these constrictions, be corrupted for a time. But sooner or later the will of the people incorruptibly finds out its true level, which is self-government, and settles into it. Self-government is not only the best government; in the profoundest sense it is the only government.

The Uncommon Man

BY

HERBERT HOOVER

FORMER PRESIDENT OF

THE UNITED STATES

"That nation is proudest and noblest and most exalted which has the greatest number of really great men."

—SINCLAIR LEWIS

RECENTLY, IN MY opinion, there has been too much talk about the Common Man. It has been dinned into us that this is the Century of the Common Man. The idea seems to be that the Common Man has come into his own at last.

Thus we are in danger of developing a cult of the Common Man, which means a cult of mediocrity. But there is at least one hopeful sign: I have never been able to find out who this Common Man is. In fact, most Americans, and especially women, will get mad and fight if you try calling them common.

This is hopeful because it shows that most people are holding fast to an essential fact in American life. We believe in equal opportunity for all, but we know that this includes the opportunity to rise to leadership—in other words, to be uncommon.

Let us remember that the great human advances have not been brought about by mediocre men and women. They were brought about by distinctly uncommon people with vital sparks of leadership. Many of the great leaders were, it is true, of humble origin, but that alone was not their greatness.

It is a curious fact that when you get sick you want an uncommon doctor; if your car breaks down you want an uncommonly good mechanic; when we get into war we want dreadfully an uncommon admiral and an uncommon general.

I have never met a father and mother who did not want their children to grow up to be uncommon men and women. May it always be so. For the future of America rests not in mediocrity, but in the constant renewal of leadership in every phase of our national life.

The Danger

BY

ALDOUS HUXLEY

NOVELIST, PHILOSOPHER,
AUTHOR OF "POINT COUNTERPOINT"

"Power tends to corrupt, and absolute power corrupts absolutely."

—LORD ACTON

THIS ONE BRIEF sentence sums up the fundamental problem of politics and economics in our time. It is simply this: How are we to avoid the concentration and consequent abuse of power?

The framers of the American Constitution did their best to solve the problem as it presented itself a hundred and seventy years ago. Since then, circumstances have changed, profoundly; but the old principles are still true. If it was bad in earlier times to give an individual or organization too much power, it is no less bad today. And yet, in recent years, the tendency has everywhere been, not to limit and disperse power, but to concentrate it into fewer and fewer hands.

The power that has been given to a few political and economic leaders must be taken back by individuals and cooperating groups. The existence of a free society depends on personal self-reliance and on institutions that embody the idea of self-government. Liberty is not compatible with laziness. To "let George do it" is to let George run the whole show. But "power tends to corrupt"; and when George is allowed to run the whole show, he soon ceases to be George and becomes another, and much less pleasant person, called Adolf or Benito.

The Heritage

BY

RALPH BARTON PERRY

PHILOSOPHER, AUTHOR OF
"PURITANISM AND DEMOCRACY"

"It is a poor heart that never rejoices."
—ANNE FREMANTLE IN "JAMES AND JOAN"

IN RECENT YEARS, we have, as Americans, become increasingly self-critical. We have been overtaken with a conviction of sin. We have converted our heroes into blunderers, our saints into self-seekers, our legends into lies, and our cheers into sneers. Ashamed of our reputation for boasting, we have taken to apologizing—to ourselves and all the world.

Let us go back to the root of the matter. Self-criticism may teach you to measure yourself more severely and more truly. But it is good to demand more of yourself only if you respond to that demand. There can be no wholehearted effort without pride—pride in the goal itself, pride in one's latent power to move forward, and even pride in the attainment.

We have swung so far towards self-abasement, that we can now recover a right balance of moral force only by a conscious recovery of pride. I would have every man be proud of what he is—proud of being old if he is old, or of being young if he is young, proud of being American, and above all proud of democracy.

I would have every American proudly confident that democracy is the best form of society that man has dreamed. That it should exist at all, and that it should have made some headway against servitude and inhumanity, is reason for pride—and reason for faith in the power of America to ascend the long, hard path that lies ahead.

Things

to

Come

Crises

BY

JOHN ERSKINE

AUTHOR, EDUCATOR

---

*"This time, like all other times, is a very good one,
if we but know what to do with it."*

— EMERSON

RALPH WALDO EMERSON spoke these words in
1837, when most of his hearers at the Harvard Phi Beta
Kappa meeting were fed up with Andrew Jackson. That
un-Harvard-like person was at the end of his second term,
having, as his critics felt, all but wrecked American society
and the foundations of national credit. In the circumstances,
Emerson went pretty far. He said that the best moment to
be born is always during a revolution; that life is just one
revolution after another, a series of crises in which we take
farewell of the past, and, if we are wise, meet the future.
Every time is a good time to live in, if we know what to
do with it.

The Goal

BY

CLIFTON FADIMAN

AUTHOR, CRITIC, QUIZ-MASTER
OF "INFORMATION, PLEASE"

"I am a citizen, not of Athens or Greece, but of the world."

—SOCRATES

THESE ARE THE words of Socrates, the ancient Greek
philosopher, and perhaps the wisest man who ever lived.
Despite his words, Socrates lived and died a good and pa-
triotic Athenian citizen. He found no conflict between the
laws of his little community and the greater laws of reason
by which all men should be governed. Today, Socrates'
words have greater force than ever. Either we must all think
of ourselves as part of mankind; or mankind will, within
our own time, sink to the level of the beast in the jungle.

Frontiers

BY

RAY LYMAN WILBUR

LATE CHANCELLOR OF STANFORD UNIVERSITY

*" . . . Come, my friends. 'Tis not too late to seek a
newer world."*

—TENNYSON

JUST A FEW years ago we heard people talking about
"no more frontiers." They said there was no more need
to fight and struggle for existence. They said we must learn
to live leisurely and to develop new habits of recreation
because machines would do so much work for us that our
principal responsibility would be to divide up the jobs of
supervising them.

Now the whole world population finds itself where it
must work harder than ever if it is to get out of the hole
that it is in. Many people and many nations face a stark
biological future—competition for breathing space, for
food, for shelter, and for the means to rear their children.
If we do not use opportunity wisely, we will get pushed

aside by other forces. The weeds stand ever ready to replace the plants.

Nature presses hard on every living cell. Each must have air, water, light, nourishment. And man cannot escape this relationship to nature. To halt, to be satisfied, is in part to die.

To live, to grow, to have a family, to seek new paths, and to help the less fortunate—these are goals to keep human beings at the top of those biological forces we call life. But we reach them through striving, not through resting. Happiness must be *achieved,* freedom must be *won,* and faith must be *sought.*

Science

BY

CHARLES F. KETTERING

SCIENTIST, INVENTOR OF THE
AUTOMOBILE IGNITION SYSTEM

*"We are reading the first verse of the first chapter
of a book whose pages are infinite. . . ."*
—UNKNOWN

I DO NOT know who wrote these words. But I have
always liked them as a reminder that the future can be anything we want to make it. We can take the mysterious, hazy
future and carve out of it anything that we can imagine,
just as a sculptor carves a statue from a shapeless stone.

We are all in the position of the farmer. If we plant
good clean seed, we reap a good harvest. If our seed is poor
and full of weeds, we reap a useless crop. If we plant
nothing at all, we harvest nothing at all.

I want to make the future to be better than the past. I
don't want it contaminated by the mistakes and errors with
which history is filled. We should all be concerned about

the future because that is where we will spend the remainder of our lives.

The past is gone and static. Nothing we do can change it. The future is before us and dynamic. Everything we do will affect it. Each day brings with it new frontiers, in our homes and in our businesses, if we will only recognize them. We are just at the beginning of progress in every field of human endeavor.

Men and Machines

BY

DAVID LILIENTHAL

FORMER CHAIRMAN OF TVA,
NOW CHAIRMAN
OF THE U. S. ATOMIC ENERGY COMMISSION

*"Underneath all, I swear nothing is good to me
now that ignores individuals."*

—WALT WHITMAN

IT IS TRUE that we cannot be starving and cold and still
be happy. But an abundance of food, the satisfaction of ele-
mentary physical needs alone, is not enough. A man wants
to feel that he is important. He wants to be able not only
to express his opinion freely, but to know that it carries
some weight; to know that there are some things that he
decides, or has a part in deciding, and that he is a needed
and useful part of something far bigger than he is.

This hankering to be an individual is probably greater
today than ever before. Huge factories, assembly lines,
mysterious mechanisms, standardization—these underline
the smallness of the individual, because they are so fatally

impersonal. If the immediate future of the world could be made personal to the life of most men; if they could see themselves, because it was true, as actual participants in that development in their own communities, on their own land, at their own jobs and businesses—there would be something to tie to. Men would not only have more things; they would be stronger and happier men.

It is the unique strength of democratic methods that they can provide a way of stimulating and releasing the individual resourcefulness and inventiveness, the pride of workmanship, the creative genius of human beings whatever their station or function. A world of science and great machines is still a world of men; our modern task is more difficult, but the opportunity for democratic methods is greater even than in the days of the ax and the hand loom.

The Problem

BY

CORDELL HULL

FORMER U. S. SECRETARY OF STATE

*"We have writing and teaching, science and power;
we have tamed the beasts and schooled the light-
ning . . . but we have still to tame ourselves."*

—H. G. WELLS

THESE WORDS FROM the "Outline of History"
might well be read today before each meeting of an international body. The peace we are striving so hard to win cannot be won by conquering one another at the peace table
any more than it can be won by conquering one another
on the battlefield. To live side by side. nations, like families
on a street, must be worthy in their own right. Each nation
must cast out selfishness, ignoble ambition, prejudice, and
the willingness to profit at the expense of any neighbor.

And we must tame ourselves; no one else can do it for
us. Peace is not a thing to be handed down. It must begin
with self-discipline—self-discipline in the individual, the

home, the nation. When all nations have geared themselves to the true principles of living, peace will no longer be a problem. Peace will suddenly be among us—as if by its own accord.

Sovereignty

BY

NICHOLAS MURRAY BUTLER

LATE PRESIDENT OF COLUMBIA UNIVERSITY

*"If there is any message that China wishes to give,
it is that we are prepared to yield if necessary a part
of our sovereignty to the new international organization—in the interest of collective security."*

—T. V. SOONG

THESE WORDS WERE spoken by China's delegate
to the United Nations Conference in San Francisco. If we
heed them, they could make a turning point in world history. For, after all, it is the exaggerated concept of national
sovereignty which has been responsible for most of the
world's wars and which darkens the future even now.

Actually, there is no Chinese crisis, no Indian crisis, no
German crisis, no American crisis; what we are facing is a
world-wide crisis which appears in different forms in each
land, different according to national conditions, national
habits, and national circumstances. It is one and the same

disease, one and the same condition, and it can only be cured in one and the same way.

The problem of the people is world-wide. The cure must be world-wide. International understanding, international cooperation, international administrative policies—and they alone—will restore health to this ailing world. Whatever any single nation may do by itself will be temporary and limited, because not even the most powerful or the largest or the richest can deal finally and satisfactorily with all today's phenomena and problems.

We have come to the time when, if liberty is to be preserved and extended, its upholders and defenders must be prepared to lead the way to the next stage of political organization. The world is waiting for a new application of the federal principle.

"Dependence Day"

BY
ILONA MASSEY
HUNGARIAN-BORN
MOTION PICTURE STAR

*"Independence? We are all dependent on one an-
other, every soul of us on earth."*
—GEORGE BERNARD SHAW

AS A NEW American, this suggestion may seem presumptuous—but I'd like to propose a new kind of holiday. I
would call it "Dependence Day."

For generations, Americans have, quite rightly, been cel-
ebrating July 4 as the day of our political independence.
But on my holiday people will think about their human
*inter*dependence.

On this day people will set aside a little time, only a few
moments perhaps, to reflect upon and give thanks for our
vital dependence upon one another. Dependents will count
their dependents. Everyone will contemplate the vast num-

ber of people he is dependent upon. It will be a day to think about our relationships as husbands and wives, parents and children, bosses and workers, city dwellers and country folk.

We will all recognize each other on Dependence Day. Passers-by will smile in greeting. Strangers—mutually dependent people who haven't been introduced—will exchange some word or sign to act out our appreciation of our dependence upon each other.

It will be a day of friendship and recognition of and for —all of us.

No guns will be fired. There will be no fireworks to mark the day, no speeches, no martial music. The observation of Dependence Day will take place in a man's own mind and heart, not in his ears. It doesn't call for signs or badges or symbols. For most of all, this will be an occasion for quiet thought.

After all, who is really "independent" today? Nobody. What person or state is truly "sovereign"? None.

The very nature of modern life means that all of us are increasingly dependent on each other. We will survive only if we can find some way to remember that fact, and act accordingly.

Maybe Dependence Day will help us to remember.

PART THREE

Man
and His
God

Beyond

the

Stars

LIGHT FROM DARKNESS BY Gerald W. Johnson
GOD OR NOTHING BY Alfred Noyes
ELDER JOHNSON SAID— BY Roark Bradford
IS THERE A MERCIFUL GOD? BY Thomas Merton

Light From Darkness

BY

GERALD W. JOHNSON

HISTORIAN AND CRITIC, AUTHOR OF
"AMERICAN HEROES AND HERO WORSHIP"

"Light that makes some things seen, makes some things invisible. Were it not for darkness and the shadow of the earth, the noblest part of the Creation would remain unseen, and the stars in heaven invisible."

—SIR THOMAS BROWNE (ADAPTED)

WHEN I, BEING then very young, first discovered this passage I was enchanted by its sound, and I still consider it one of the finest examples of rolling thunder to be found in English prose. But living through two wars and a depression has battered into my head realization that there is more than resonance in the old Doctor's words.

Thomas Browne was a great man who lived in a great period, and this passage gives a clue as to why he and his

147

time were great. Like us, he lived in a perplexing age, when the boundaries of knowledge were being suddenly expanded and the old learning was proving less and less adequate. But he was not afraid.

Knowing that he knew nothing, he had the heart to believe that what his ignorance concealed from him was not terrible, but finer than anything so far discovered, and he dared push forward into all truth. For, suspecting that his light was in reality but shadow, he was confident that beyond the shadow he would find God.

Not even the atomic bomb could have frightened that man; and with his courage we, too, might be great.

God or Nothing

BY

ALFRED NOYES

POET AND AUTHOR

"The sun, which has all those planets revolving around it and dependent upon it, can ripen a bunch of grapes as if it had nothing else in the world to do."

—GALILEO

THIS WAS GALILEO'S answer to those who attacked him when he said that the Earth was not the center of the universe. His system, the critics said, made human beings insignificant.

Galileo's answer, made three hundred years ago, is a source of strength in our time. For today many of us again feel that the individual is insignificant in the immense universe of modern science. But if the physical Sun can be so responsible for the minutest flower in the field, there is certainly no reason to feel that there is any limit to the scope of that central Power, which created all the suns, all life, all spiritual values and the spirit of man himself.

Behind Galileo's defense was his own belief that the Universe is centered on neither the Earth nor the Sun—it is centered on either God or nothing. If the latter, there can be no real belief, no sensible philosophy. Out of this blind alley, he turns naturally to the other alternative—God. Galileo's words, the first voice of modern science, call us back to faith, hope and true belief.

Elder Johnson Said—

BY

ROARK BRADFORD

AUTHOR OF
"OLD MAN ADAM AND HIS CHILLUN"

"If you don't believe in God, you ain't a whole man; you just a number in the book. A lot of smart people claim they don't believe nothin' unless they can see it. Look, friend, you can't see electricity in that high-tension wire up yonder, but I DARE YOU TO TOUCH IT! No, you can't see that electricity but you can see the light."

—ELDER JOHNSON

THE ABOVE IS an excerpt from a sermon by Elder J. J. Johnson, pastor of Sunlight Christian Spiritual Mission African Baptist Church in New Orleans. It is a slap at the Sophists, of whom he has never heard, and an expression of a faith, of which he has an abundance. It is true that Plato took the Sophists apart and affirmed the existence of God with a more orderly logic than Elder Johnson's. It is true that the prophet Ezekiel denounced unbelievers and pictured God's presence in more flamboyant language. The idea of a Supreme Being is as old as mankind, and in all ages wise men have worked to justify it.

Yet, when some of my intellectual friends, who have faith in nothing except their own ideologies, begin to solve the world's problems, I always think of Elder Johnson's sermon. He can scarcely read and write, but he has lots of faith and he has solved many problems for himself and for his congregation. Elder Johnson is more than a number in the book. I think he is a whole man.

Is There a Merciful God?

BY

THOMAS MERTON

INTELLECTUAL-TURNED-TRAPPIST MONK
AUTHOR OF "THE SEVEN STOREY MOUNTAIN"

"But the Lord delayeth not his promise, as some imagine, but dealeth patiently for your sake, not willing that any should perish, but that all should return to penance."

—II PETER, 3:9

IT IS ONLY the infinite mercy and love of God that has prevented us from tearing ourselves to pieces and destroying His entire creation long ago. People seem to think that it is in some way proof that no merciful God exists, if we have so many wars. On the contrary, consider how in spite of centuries of sin and greed and lust and cruelty and hatred and avarice and oppression and injustice, spawned and bred by the free wills of men, the human race can still recover, each time, and can still produce men and women who overcome evil with good, hatred with love, greed with charity, lust and cruelty with sanctity. How could all this be possible without the merciful love of God, pouring out His grace upon us? Can there be any doubt where wars come from and where peace comes from, when the children of this world, excluding God from their peace conferences, only manage to bring about greater and greater wars the more they talk about peace?

There is not a flower that opens, not a seed that falls into the ground, and not an ear of wheat that nods on the end of its stalk in the wind that does not preach and proclaim the greatness and the mercy of God to the whole world.

There is not an act of kindness or generosity, not an act of sacrifice done, or a word of peace and gentleness spoken, not a child's prayer uttered, that does not sing hymns to God before His throne, and in the eyes of men, and before their faces.

How does it happen that in the thousands of generations of murderers since Cain, our dark bloodthirsty ancestor, that some of us can still be saints? The quietness and hiddenness and placidity of the truly good people in the world all proclaim the glory of God.

All creatures, every graceful movement, every ordered act of the human will, all are sent to us as prophets from God. But because of our stubbornness they come to us only to blind us further.

God's

World

On Peace of Mind

BY

JOSHUA LOTH LIEBMAN

CLERGYMAN AND AUTHOR OF
"PEACE OF MIND"

*"On my head pour only the sweet waters of serenity.
Give me the gift of the Untroubled Mind."*

ONCE, AS a young man full of exuberant fancy, I under-
took to draw up a catalogue of the acknowledged "goods"
of life. As other men sometimes tabulate lists of properties
they own or would like to own, I set down my inventory of
earthly desirables: health, love, beauty, talent, power,
riches, and fame.

When my inventory was completed I proudly showed it
to a wise elder who had been the mentor and spiritual model
of my youth. Perhaps I was trying to impress him with my
precocious wisdom. Anyway, I handed him the list. "This,"
I told him confidently, "is the sum of mortal goods. Could
a man possess them all, he would be as a god."

At the corners of my friend's old eyes, I saw wrinkles of

amusement gathering in a patient net. "An excellent list," he said, pondering it thoughtfully. "Well digested in content and set down in not-unreasonable order. But it appears, my young friend, that you have omitted the most important element of all. You have forgotten the one ingredient, lacking which each possession becomes a hideous torment."

"And what," I asked, peppering my voice with truculence, "is that missing ingredient?"

With a pencil stub he crossed out my entire schedule. Then, having demolished my adolescent dream structure at a single stroke, he wrote down three syllables: peace of mind. "This is the gift that God reserves for His special protégés," he said.

"Talent and beauty He gives to many. Wealth is commonplace, fame not rare. But peace of mind—that is His final guerdon of approval, the fondest insignia of His love. He bestows it charily. Most men are never blessed with it; others wait all their lives—yes, far into advanced age—for this gift to descend upon them."

He scanned the doubt on my young forehead. "This is no private opinion of mine," he explained. "I am merely paraphrasing from the Psalmists, Marcus Aurelius, and Lao-tse. 'God,' says each of these wise ones, 'heaps worldly gifts at the feet of foolish men. But on my head pour only the sweet waters of serenity. Give me the gift of the Untroubled Mind.'"

On Love

BY

MARJORIE KINNAN RAWLINGS

AUTHOR OF "THE YEARLING"

"Though I speak with the tongues of men and of angels, and have not love, I am become as sounding brass, or a tinkling cymbal.

"And though I have the gift of prophecy, and understand all mysteries, and all knowledge; and though I have all faith, so that I could remove mountains, and have not love, I am nothing."
— I CORINTHIANS 13:1-2

THE ANCIENT WORDS of Paul have always seemed to me to hold the complete answer to all of human living. Man, in his struggle out of the prehistoric mire, becomes proud and arrogant with each new step of progress. He becomes wise and clever. Surely, we must match each pace forward with a corresponding love, or compassion, or understanding, else we perish. We stand at a moment in human history when, to survive, we must choose between love or hate. "And now abideth faith, hope and love, but the greatest of these is love."

The Fatherhood of God

BY

CLARE BOOTHE LUCE

AUTHOR, PLAYWRIGHT,
FORMER MEMBER OF CONGRESS

". . . this nation, under God, shall have a new birth of freedom . . ."

—ABRAHAM LINCOLN

OUR OWN DOCTRINE of natural rights, set forth in the Constitution and Declaration of Independence, holds that each and every one of us—regardless of color, creed or birth—has certain inalienable rights. They are inalienable for one reason only: because they are the endowment of the Creator.

If the day ever comes when the men and women of our Western Civilization desert completely the historic concept of man as a child of God with free will and an immortal soul—if the day comes, in short, when we, too, go over to "scientific materialism"—on that day not all our oil or gold in the ground, nor our assembly lines, nor our air forces nor our navies, nor even our sole possession of the atomic bomb, shall save us. On that day freedom would perish in the totalitarian night of the world. Lincoln was right to remind us that it is only *under God* that this nation, or any nation, can be free.

The Brotherhood of Man

BY

HARRY EMERSON FOSDICK

CLERGYMAN AND WRITER

"We cannot make a heaven in our own country and leave a hell outside."
—CLEMENT ATTLEE

PRIME MINISTER ATTLEE said these words—and they are the pith of the world's problem. Even in public health we cannot have the hell of epidemics elsewhere and be safe ourselves. As for war, when the flood breaks loose no isolation can keep any great nation out, with atomic ruin stopping at its peaceful border. If we have peace now it must be world peace; if we have economic security in one hemisphere, economic chaos must not ravage the other.

Like it or not, we are members one of another; mankind is no longer pigeonholed in isolated compartments. We may as well face the truth. We live in one world now, headed together for heaven or hell on earth.

World Without End

BY

BRUCE MARSHALL

ACCOUNTANT-TURNED-WRITER, AUTHOR
OF "FATHER MALACHY'S MIRACLE" AND
"THE WORLD, THE FLESH AND FATHER SMITH"

*" . . . The moving waters at their priest-like task
Of pure ablution round earth's human shores. . . ."*
—KEATS

I THINK OFTEN of these lines, both when I am
sad and when I am glad. I think of them when I am sad,
because their rhythm teaches me that the timeless patience
of God is reflected in the mirror of the sea. Whatever the
stupidities of men in cities or council chambers, the waves
will always be in choir, chanting their psalm. They sang
before Genghis Khan and they will still sing after the atom
bomb. Those thoughts make me glad and I murmur the
words again, because I am also grateful.

10

Valley

and

Shadow

On Facing Life by Dorothy Van Doren
On Facing Death by Adela Rogers St. Johns
On Eternity by George and Helen Papashvily

On Facing Life

BY

DOROTHY VAN DOREN

EDITOR AND AUTHOR

"I would finish hoeing my garden."
—ST. FRANCIS OF ASSISI

THESE WORDS WERE St. Francis' answer when someone asked him, while working in his garden, what he would do if he were suddenly to learn that he would die at sunset that day.

They seem to me an answer to all the troubled young people these days who are beginning life in a world that appears to hold no security for them or for anyone, young or old.

Why should they bother to go to college when the atom war is just around the corner? Why should a young wife have a baby when the ceiling may collapse on its crib? Why should one paint a picture or write a song or begin a novel?

On Facing Life

We can't be sure of anything, these young people say, not now, or next year or the year after that. Why should we try to make a life for ourselves, they ask. Why should we go to classes or take examinations or get married or look for an apartment or try for a job? Next spring, or some spring too frighteningly near, it may all go, the life we have begun. Our world is in deadly peril, we have lost the promise of tomorrow.

St. Francis put the answer in a simple metaphor: go on hoeing your garden. The task is still here—the house to build, the book to write, the examination to prepare for. If the future looks dark, so did it on the morning before the first Christmas—and in the year 5,000 B.C. And however dark it seems today, however dark it is, we shall meet life better if we have fulfilled the present to the best of our ability. Today is still ours, along with the obligation to live it to the full. As St. Francis said, we must go on hoeing our garden.

On Facing Death

BY

ADELA ROGERS ST. JOHNS

NOVELIST AND MAGAZINE WRITER

"Grow old along with me!
The best is yet to be,
The last of life, for which the first was made."
—ROBERT BROWNING

NOTHING IS SADDER than not to know the truth of Browning's words; nothing is more rewarding than living by them. There is as much of the "last of life" to live as the first, maybe more. So, accept the blessed idea that the best is yet to be, and you will live a rich, full span on this earth, wasting none of it in future fears or vain regrets. But if the last of life is to be a serene and wonderful time beyond all other, the first must be planned.

Many strong, fine, exciting things belong to youth. I'm glad I missed none of them. But they pass out of our experience in due time and we must be ready to let them go and take others just as good, or better. There are those who store nothing in these splendid, reckless young years to fill the later ones. They think of happiness in terms of what youth alone can be, and know and do. For them, the last of life can be barren, cold, sometimes ugly in its attempts to prolong that youth.

Those who plant seeds of love, service, friendship, know the last of life as a privilege, and a continuing adventure. The fevers of the blood die down, the spirit grows serene. Friendships grow holier with shared years. Memories become hallowed. Beauty can be enjoyed without the torturing need for possession. Humor becomes part of wisdom. And service is a gift worth offering to those still on the battlefield of youth. The harvest of work well done, of love freely given, is ripe for reaping. The books we never had time to read, the music we never had time to hear, the people we never had time to talk to, the games we never watched because we were so busy playing them, the prayers we never had time to say, the God we never had time to know—all these can be ours at last. And when that chapter ends, surely the Best of All is—yet to be.

On Eternity

BY

GEORGE AND HELEN PAPASHVILY

AUTHORS OF "ANYTHING CAN HAPPEN"

"This minute, too, is part of eternity."

WHEN GEORGE WAS a little boy in the Caucasus he was taken once to visit a revered old man who lived all alone, high on a mountain top.

It was customary for each child in the district to give the hermit a gift and receive in return a special proverb or word of advice that he might use as a talisman thereafter through his future life.

The old man had a stern face and a long white beard. He beckoned the boy to come closer. George was frightened but he went. The old man waved the grown people away and then grew friendly. He asked the little boy at his side what he wanted to do and where he wanted to go when he was grown. He told him tales of his own life and his travels over the earth.

After a little while he said, "Now to give you your proverb. I want it to be something that will be of use to you when you are young and when you are old—something to help when you feel sad or tired or discouraged—something to remember when you doubt and fear."

George waited.

The old man bent down and whispered in his ear, "This minute, too, is part of eternity."

George didn't understand it (perhaps he wasn't meant to) until he grew up. For like many simple truths it needs thought and reflection and experience to make it clear.

But once comprehended it affords a whole new perspective of life with vistas as wide as space and as long as time. The simplest act acquires dignity and import; the most fleeting moment, meaning. Birth and death, instead of being two irreconcilable parts, form a harmonious whole.

11

Alone

with

God

WHEN LINCOLN PRAYED BY Robert I. Gannon, S. J.
THE MOOD BY Lily Pons
THE KEY BY Louis Bromfield
THE PERFECT PRAYER BY St. Francis of Assisi

When Lincoln Prayed

BY

ROBERT I. GANNON, S. J.

FORMER PRESIDENT, FORDHAM UNIVERSITY

"God hath given to a man that is good in his sight,
wisdom and knowledge and joy . . ."
—ECCLESIASTES 2:26

THIS IS A story which almost tells itself. It happened during the early hours of the Battle of Gettysburg. In the White House, Abraham Lincoln was pacing up and down, lonely and troubled, as the battle reports poured in and the fate of the United States hung in the balance.

At that time, when everybody seemed panic-stricken, Lincoln went to his room and locked the door. One can picture him there, down on his knees, his great head in his hands, praying like a child. Later, Lincoln described that moment to a friend in this fashion:

"I told God that I had done all that I could and that now the result was in His hands; that if this country was to be saved, it was because He so willed it! The burden rolled off my shoulders. My intense anxiety was relieved and in its place came a great trustfulness!"

It isn't necessary to say very much in comment on this story. It stands by itself, a reminder that now, as in all times of crisis, there is an enduring source of strength and consolation—if only we have the will and the wisdom to turn toward it.

The Mood

BY

LILY PONS

OPERA STAR

"The ideal man is his own best friend and takes delight in privacy."

—ARISTOTLE

AMERICAN PEOPLE ARE becoming more and more like the Red Queen in "Alice in Wonderland," who had to keep running in order to stay where she was. The hectic tempo and mass activity of the business world have spread into all phases of modern life. People have forgotten how to slow down, how to be alone.

How often, during the furious activity of the week, we think of all the things we will accomplish on the week end . . . reading a book we have long heard about, taking care of unfinished correspondence, putting our houses—literally and figuratively—in order. But when the week end arrives, we find ourselves hurrying to parties to which we do not really want to go, being swept up by a dozen social obligations. Finally there is nothing left to the week end but the beginning of another working week.

But the "ideal man" whom Aristotle described, indeed, the healthy man in this or any other generation, allows himself some time for his own thoughts. He is able to behave as a social being when he is in society, but he is not afraid of his own company. He knows that each day he must give some time to contemplation—that is, to looking over his actions of the day and comparing them with his intentions, making constructive plans for the future and simply being himself.

The problem, of course, is where to find the time or the place to be alone. Singers and musicians are fortunate, for their work compels them to take time to study and practice, and time to rest before performances or concerts.

If musicians find such relaxation a help, then I think men and women in the business world would too. Take a little time before that next conference to let your mind run away from office cares. Break the boredom of a routine job, now and then, with a few minutes of "escape" thinking. If you have time left over after lunch, take a walk and let your mind be free—perhaps for a daydream, perhaps for a prayer.

Privacy of this sort can be found by any man. And each of us must find it if he is to remain a consistent and sane individual with a normal, happy inner life.

The Key

BY
LOUIS BROMFIELD

AUTHOR OF "THE GREEN BAY TREE"
AND "THE RAINS CAME"

"He prayeth best who loveth best
All things both great and small;
For the dear God who loveth us,
He made and loveth all."
—COLERIDGE

THESE LINES COME from one of the most beautiful poems ever written. They have in them deep philosophic implications, both for the individual and for the world. In their simple beauty lies the essence of Christ's teachings. Indeed, of every great religion. They represent the spiritual satisfaction without which any career, however successful in a worldly sense, is a sterile and frustrated business.

Lacking the fundamental philosophy of love expressed in these lines, the life of man becomes little more than a brutish adventure in time—and the peace and unity of nations little more than a dream and a delusion.

The Perfect Prayer

BY

ST. FRANCIS OF ASSISI

The prayer which follows was selected by Albert L. Cox, lawyer, of Washington, D. C. We print it here as a summing up. Even though St. Francis' prayer was written 700 years ago, it reflects, simply, beautifully, and completely, the many facets of philosophy in the preceding selections. In short, it expresses a way of life for our times—and for all time:

Lord, make me an instrument of Thy Peace. Where there is hatred, let me sow love. Where there is injury, pardon. Where there is doubt, faith. Where there is despair, hope. Where there is darkness, light. Where there is sadness, joy.

O Divine Master, grant that I may not so

much seek to be consoled as to console; to be understood, as to understand; to be loved, as to love; for it is in giving that we receive, it is in pardoning that we are pardoned, and it is in dying that we are born to Eternal Life.

Of all the selections published in "This Week" none brought as great a response as this prayer. The following letter is typical:

"Last Christmas you printed a prayer by St. Francis of Assisi. At that time life looked glum to me. That prayer hit me between the eyes. I cut it out of the magazine and thumb-tacked it to the pine-paneled wall in our living room. I read it over and over, and finally put it to a test. I lived by those words for one brief week and found the most tremendous joy and peace. I am still living, gloriously, by them."

PART FOUR

Philosophy
in the
Making

Here the Reader
May Join With Sixteen Others
In His Quest for
Words to Live By

The Arch

BY

IRWIN EDMAN

PHILOSOPHER AND AUTHOR OF
"PHILOSOPHER'S QUEST"

"Yet all experience is an arch wherethro'
Gleams that untravell'd world whose margin fades
For ever and for ever when I move."
—TENNYSON

WHEN I WAS very young I thought that some day I should arrive at a fixed and final version of the truth, lighting upon it in the pages of a book or in some sudden bright new page of life. But as one grows older the force of Tennyson's words grows stronger. Before one lies an untraveled realm and a constantly changing one. The world appears different at fifty than it did at twenty, or one has learned nothing. And if the world looks different to the same mind at two periods of a man's life, by the same token it looks and must look different to different persons even in the same era.

In this book a group of contemporaries have made com-

Irwin Edman

ments on quotations that have been for each of them words to live by. Each man, of course, must ultimately live by his own words in his own way and see nature and man through his own arch of experience. But it is the same world we all live in, and essentially the same human nature we share. That is why communication is possible and why we can learn from each other's experience. A philosophy is inevitably the result of one man's temperament and history. But any man's world-view becomes more generous and imaginative and liberated when he succeeds, if only for the time being, in seeing through the eyes of others and vicariously sharing their quest.

These words by Irwin Edman form a perfect introduction to this final section.

So far, the selections have been grouped in an ordered pattern to show the range of thoughts and emotions which make up a mature and happy Way of Life.

But the following pages, more or less at random, are comments from men and women in many walks of life. They help make the point that each of us has something to say; each makes his contribution to the mosaic. And that applies to you, too. It is for this reason that the final page in this book is reserved for some great and simple words that bring you particular inspiration—in short, your own Words to Live By. On that page, my work as editor will end, and it will be for you to join in the quest.

THE EDITOR

An Actress
GERTRUDE LAWRENCE
STAGE AND RADIO STAR

"God pays debts without money."
—MRS. JANE BANKS

THIS WAS ONE of my grandmother's favorite sayings. She used it constantly and with such consummate confidence that it never occurred to me to doubt its truth,
although it was many years before I was old enough to
understand its great depth of meaning. What an immense
amount of comfort is packed into those five words!

What need is there to fret or worry or scheme? For God
may be trusted to repay what you sincerely, and humbly,
believe life owes you for work well down, for fortitude in
disappointment, for responsibilities well shouldered, for
patience and perseverance in the face of apparent failure.

Be patient; the debt will be paid you in His own good
time, and with interest. I have always found this to be so.

My grandmother's philosophy, which she shared with
me when I was still a child, has helped me over many a
rough and stony path, and always will.

An Admiral
WILLIAM F. HALSEY
FLEET ADMIRAL, U.S.N., RETIRED

*"No Captain can do very wrong if he places his
Ship alongside that of an Enemy."*
—HORATIO NELSON

ADMIRAL NELSON WROTE these words in a
memorandum to his officers on October 9, 1805. Twelve
days later he was killed aboard his flagship at the Battle
of Trafalgar, in the hour of his greatest victory.

The detection devices and long-range weapons of modern warfare have made it almost impossible for a captain
to heed Nelson literally; but no device can prevent a man
from heeding the spirit of Nelson's counsel.

That the best defense is a strong offense is a military
principle, but its application is wider than war. All problems, personal, national, or combat, become smaller if you
don't dodge them. Touch a thistle timidly, and it pricks
you; grasp it boldly, and its spines crumble. Carry the battle
to the enemy! Lay your ship alongside his!

An Ambassador
LORD HALIFAX
FORMER BRITISH AMBASSADOR TO THE U. S.

"Service is the rent we pay for our room on earth."

THESE ARE WORDS which, if I remember them correctly, are used at the meetings of "Toc H," a society organized by British servicemen in the Ypres salient during the First World War. From the first time I heard them, they made a profound impression on me.

We have been too much inclined to let our thoughts rest upon what we judge to be our rights, without giving equal weight to the recognition of our duties. But in these words the balance is set right, and the claim is made on every one of us to serve our fellows.

There is no room in the modern world for easy indifference to the world's needs: we are all our "brother's keeper." Only by translating this truth into terms of daily life can we hope to establish true understanding between men and nations—and make the world more worthy of all the sacrifice that twice in a generation has been spent to save it.

A Doctor

LORD MORAN

PRESIDENT OF THE BRITISH ROYAL COLLEGE
OF PHYSICIANS

"The thing in the world I am most afraid of is fear."

—MONTAIGNE

TWICE IN MY lifetime I have seen boys grow to men, only to be consumed by war, and I have come to think about this almost every day. My conclusion is that fortitude in war has its roots in the morality of peace, for courage is not a chance gift of Nature like an aptitude for games.

A man of courage in war is a man of character in peace. And character, as Aristotle taught, is a habit, the daily choice between right and wrong. It is a quality which grows to maturity, so that where courage is concerned the boy is father to the man, and the bearing of an army provides a census of the character of the nation. In the long run a nation finds its strongest defense lines lie back in home and school, where character is built. That is what gives free people the power to win their freedom—and to hold it.

A Business Man
DANIEL STARCH
BUSINESS RESEARCH CONSULTANT

I HAVE LONG been a collector of Words to Live By. As a statistician, I was anxious to know which sayings are most highly valued by Americans as a whole. So I worked out a "Words to Live By Survey." It began with a list of nearly one hundred famous sayings. This was then submitted to a sufficient number of selected persons throughout the country to give a cross-section opinion.

Here are the results of the poll, in order of preference, with the actual number of votes shown on the right. The sources given below are the earliest or the most widely known:

1. *Do unto others as you would that they should do unto you.*   *1,237*
2. *Know thyself.*   *1,125*
3. *Anything that is worth doing at all is worth doing well.*   *744*
4. *If at first you don't succeed, try, try again.*   *719*
5. *The great essentials of happiness are something to do, something to love, and something to hope for.*   *697*
6. *The only way to have a friend is to be one.*   *637*

7. *As a man thinketh in his heart, so is he.* 615
8. *Knowledge is power.* 615
9. *Actions speak louder than words.* 579
10. *An ounce of prevention is worth a pound of cure.* · 564

SOURCES: *1. Bible (paraphrase of Matthew and Luke). 2. Attributed originally to Socrates. 3. Earl of Chesterfield. 4. William E. Hickson. 5. Unknown. 6. Ralph Waldo Emerson. 7. Bible (Proverbs). 8. Thomas Hobbes. 9. An ancient proverb, source unknown. 10. An old English proverb.*

A General
DWIGHT D. EISENHOWER
FORMER CHIEF OF STAFF, U.S.A.

"The discipline which makes the soldiers of a free country reliable in battle is not to be gained by harsh or tyrannical treatment. On the contrary, such treatment is far more likely to destroy than to make an army. It is possible to give commands in such manner as to inspire an intense desire to obey; while the opposite manner cannot fail to excite strong resentment and a desire to disobey."
—MAJOR GENERAL JOHN M. SCHOFIELD

THE WORDS ABOVE have meaning to every man who has ever served in the armed forces of the United States. They express the spirit which should always guide the leaders in the armies of a free nation. They were first spoken in an address at West Point in August, 1887. By the time I was a cadet in 1911 they had been cast on a bronze tablet at an entrance to old South Barracks where they could be seen daily by passing cadets—and every plebe was required to memorize them. These are, literally, the "Words to Live By" of the U. S. Army, and the great leaders are the ones who have lived up to them.

A Humorist
FRANKLIN P. ADAMS
COLUMNIST AND QUIZ-EXPERT

"My Son, if sinners entice thee, consent thou not."
—PROVERBS I : 10

AS A BOY, although I learned that Proverb, it seemed academic; I knew no sinners. But in 1903, I became a newspaperman. Sinners began enticing me, but I consented not. Incidentally, I didn't want to lose my job.

Then, years later, it came in handy again: When my most gregarious son was at boarding school, his marks were poor. He explained: "I just can't tell the boys to get out of my room—that I have to study." So I wrote the minister, and asked him to use that Proverb as a text. "Mr. Tileston," my boy wrote, "preached a wonderful sermon. It was 'My Son, if sinners entice thee, consent thou not.' It changed my whole attitude. I am going to consent not, and throw the boys out of my room."

A Mother
ADELINE BULLOCK

"To be a mother of men, a woman must make men of her boys. She demands their best, not because it belongs to her, but because it is due to them. For that which is due children is not ease and luxury but hardening of muscles, the habit of work, a sense of honor, and a self-respect born of integrity."
—UNKNOWN

MINE IS AN unknown name. I'm no author, journalist or actor. I am just an American housewife and mother.

From my scrapbook I give you these "Words to Live By"—author unknown. Years ago I clipped them from a newspaper. I believe that in their wisdom lies the keynote of that better world of tomorrow we hear so much about.

We mothers must recognize and accept a large portion of the responsibility of forming tomorrow's world. Let us plant so deeply in the hearts of our youth the seeds of tolerance and respect, of honor and integrity, that a better world will come, not from the fear of atomic destruction, but as a natural harvest of our thoughtful planting.

A Novelist
SINCLAIR LEWIS
NOBEL PRIZE-WINNER

IT IS HEALTHY for one's sense of noble prose to
quote the great words of a Thoreau, a Lincoln, a Plato—
yet for guidance in living, those words frequently boil
down to nothing more novel than "Be decent and generous,
and the world and you will be happier." But you cannot
be decent, you certainly cannot be generous to other people
in their way, unless you have a mature imagination. And
neither the sagest advice nor the whole cyclopedia of facts
will cultivate that imagination as will these lines of poetry
which are pure magic:

> *"A rose-red city, half as old as time."*
> —JOHN WILLIAM BURGON, "PETRA"

> *" . . . delight of battle with my peers*
> *Far on the ringing plains of windy Troy."*
> —TENNYSON, "ULYSSES"

> *"Charm'd magic casements, opening on the foam*
> *Of perilous seas, in faery lands forlorn."*
> —KEATS, "ODE TO A NIGHTINGALE"

Sinclair Lewis

"A savage place! as holy and enchanted
As e'er beneath a waning moon was haunted
By woman wailing for her demon lover!"
—COLERIDGE, "KUBLA KHAN"

Lines like these can never be too familiar! If you read them often enough to comprehend them, they are enchantments which lead on your imagination so that it perceives not only your own street, but all the streets and valleys and oceans in the world. They are keys that open the minds of all men—when you have learned how to turn them. It does not vastly matter whether you "know what they mean." Like music, they mean something beyond words and sense —something emotional and holy—and in the atomic age we need such holiness as well as the shrewdness of Franklin, the courage of Jefferson.

A Newspaperman

JOHN KIERAN

JOURNALIST, SPORTSMAN, NATURALIST

"I went to the woods because I wished to live delib-
erately, to front only the essential facts of life and
see if I could not learn what it had to teach, and not,
when I came to die, discover that I had not lived....
Let your affairs be as two or three, and not a hun-
dred or a thousand; instead of a million count half
a dozen, and keep your accounts on your thumb
nail...."

—THOREAU

EVERY SO OFTEN I feel the urge to thumb through
Thoreau's *Walden*. I do it to make sure that I am keeping
my mental feet on the ground in the general confusion that
grips the world today.

Of course, there are other reasons for reading *Walden*,
but an occasional dose of Henry David Thoreau's ax-like
logic as applied to the problem of living is a tonic that
helps me no little in these bewildering days. The lines
above have always struck me with extra force. They are
some of the first I underscored in my now well-worn copy
of Thoreau's masterpiece.

A Playwright
GEORGE BERNARD SHAW
ONE OF THE GREATEST LIVING WRITERS, AND ALWAYS A VIOLENT CRITIC OF THE FOLLIES OF HIS FELLOW MEN

THE WORLD CANNOT live by words. Confucius and Plato said the best that mortal man can say; and it had probably been said centuries before their time. From Jefferson to Franklin Roosevelt, with Longfellow, Emerson and his Boston set in between, their words have echoed in America and left us the thinly veneered savages we are. Jesus preached very eloquently that as two blacks do not make a white we had better give up punishment and revenge; but our criminal codes are none the less so barbarous that the most merciful of their implements are the electric chair and the guillotine.

Our Bibles, Korans, Vedas, Talmuds and their like are full of the wisest words; but we print them cheek by jowl with the crudest tribal idolatries; and it is on the idolatries that we act and teach our children, using the rest only to pretend we are civilized.

Ignorance, ignorance, ignorance, everywhere; that is what is wrong with us, and what defeats our good intentions every time.

What we need is not verbal wisdom; for we are stuffed with it, but knowledge of the world we are living in. The uneducated are those who have least to unlearn. When they are all thoroughly schooled our ruin will be complete.

A Poet
JOSEPH AUSLANDER
POET AND AUTHOR

"A rainbow is as real as a derrick."
—RICHARD LE GALLIENNE

IN A WORLD of jittery material values, it is wholesome to anchor our souls to the fact that there are certain things which do not change, which cannot be bought and sold over the counter, which have never gone off the gold standard, namely, God and nature and the virtues of the human heart.

Grant that the machine is formidable and efficient; that it does the work of many men; that it can lift mountains. Yet it cannot feed man's immortal longings, redeem him from despair, or answer any of his questions. These require faith and hope and courage—which, having no weight in themselves, can lift more than mountains, for they can lift the heavy human heart.

A Scientist

JULIAN HUXLEY

FORMER DIRECTOR-GENERAL

OF UNESCO

*"A community cannot be happy in one part and
unhappy in another. It's all or nothing, no patching
any more for ever."*

—H. G. WELLS

WHEN I CAME across these words in *Kipps*—a novel
written in 1905—I thought how prophetic they were. And
not only in terms of happiness, but also of morality. The
shrinkage of the world has imposed new moral duties upon
all of us. Today we can no longer continue to tolerate that
any human being anywhere on earth should suffer from
undernourishment or preventable disease or grinding pov-
erty . . . should remain ignorant or illiterate. To do so
is not merely stupid and inefficient; it is immoral and
wrong.

We need a new universal morality to replace our current
morality of nationalism and competition: If we do not
learn and practice this, we shall never get the One World
which is necessary for further human progress.

A Singer
LAURITZ MELCHIOR
THE METROPOLITAN OPERA'S
GREAT WAGNERIAN TENOR

"Let all live as they would die."
—GEORGE HERBERT

SO MANY OF us today are searching for a pattern of life that will be soul-satisfying, and free of the gnawing fear that we are frittering away our days on empty nothingness. But these words, by the English poet, George Herbert, help us overcome such fears.

The name we leave behind us is the accumulation of all the big and little things we have done during our lifetime. If we would die great, everything we do, down to the very smallest detail, must also be great.

Each of us has something different to contribute, and no matter how small or insignificant it may seem, it can be for the benefit of all. If we follow this precept constantly, we can be sure that when death comes we will be fully satisfied with the way we have lived.

203

A Statesman

W. L. MACKENZIE KING

FORMER PRIME MINISTER OF CANADA

"Over all nations is humanity."
—GOLDWIN SMITH

THE TRUTH EXPRESSED in these words lies, I believe, at the very heart of all successful reconstruction in our day. In the past, human beings have too often been the servant, not the master, of the machine; Property, too, has been regarded as more sacred than Personality; and Wealth as of greater concern than Well-Being.

Most present-day social movements have as their underlying motive the creation of a new social order. In the new social order, the emphasis placed heretofore upon *material* values will hereafter be placed upon *human* values.

Similarly, in the solution of world problems there must be increased emphasis on humanity as contrasted with nationality. Too often, in the past, nationality has been made an end in itself. Humanity's needs have been wholly subordinate. Only as nationality comes to serve humanity can we substitute co-operation for conflict.

My Own Words to Live By

BY

THE READER

Index of Quotations

Index of Contributors